Magnificent Marriage

Magnificent Marriage

10 Beacons
Show the Way
To
Marriage Happiness

DR. NICK STINNETT
DR. DONNIE HILLIARD
NANCY STINNETT

PILLAR
PRESS

Published by Pillar Press
5345 Atlanta Highway
Montgomery, Alabama 36109

Library of Congress Cataloging-in-Publication Data

Stinnett, Nick

Magnificent Marriage: 10 Beacons Show the Way to Marriage Happiness/ Nick Stinnett, Donnie Hilliard, and Nancy Stinnett

     p. cm.
   Includes appendices.

   1. Marriage – United States. 2. Family – United States.
   3. Communication – United States. 4. Interpersonal relations – United States.

ISBN 0-9700732-0-8

Special Production Assistance by Ann Fulmer, Ruby Jones, and Peggy McFarlin
Design by George Pudzis, The Graphics Factory, Inc., Montgomery, AL

Printed in the United States of America

May 2000

Acknowledgments

W e wish to express our great appreciation to the Cloverdale Center for Family Strengths, Faulkner University, and to The University of Alabama for the wonderful support which made this project possible. We are grateful for the special encouragement and support we have received from: Dr. Judy Bonner, Dean of the College of Human Environmental Sciences at The University of Alabama; Dr. Stephen Thoma, Head of the Department of Human Development and Family Studies at The University of Alabama; Dr. Billy Hilyer, President, Faulkner University; and Dr. Cecil May, Dean of the V.P. Black College of Biblical Studies at Faulkner University.

Dedicated with love

to our families and friends

and with gratitude

to the couples of the

Marriage Success Research Project

Contents

EDITORIAL NOTE: You hold in your hands the wisdom of 6,000 successful marriages, representing over 90,000 years of experience. Through this book you have the unique opportunity to learn from these couples as they share their secrets of success. They will teach you not how marriages fail but how they succeed. With the information in this book you can take the guess work out of building a happy marriage and focus your energy and efforts on what really works. It is our sincere hope that this book will be a blessing to you and that the relationship between you and your spouse becomes all that it can be – a Magnificent Marriage!

INTRODUCTION:

A Lighthouse For Your Marriage Voyage

Imagine yourself on a ship. Your voyage is taking you across a beautiful, turquoise blue sea. A pleasant breeze touches your face, giving a sense of exhilaration. The smell of salt water leaves you with the anticipation of fresh seafood. Your eyes feast on the majesty of a school of dolphins swimming graciously beside the ship. You listen to a chorus of sea gulls. You are not in a hurry. You are relaxed. You are simply savoring the beauty, peace, and adventure of each moment. You come to an enchanting island filled with beautiful flowers and waterfalls. You stop awhile to leisurely explore the island.

In a very real way your marriage is a ship and you and your loved one are on a voyage together. What kind of journey do you want it to be? It can be a voyage of beauty, joy, love, peace and adventure. If it has not been a good voyage in the past, you can change course and make the rest of the journey one of fulfillment and happiness. This book is about how you can chart your marriage destiny for success.

Of all the things that make life worthwhile, few equal the importance of the relationships we have with others. They determine and are a reflection of how we love and are loved. The quality of our marriage relationship is of paramount significance in terms of the happiness we attain in life.

WONDERFUL TRUTH

Your marriage relationship is filled with powerful strengths. These strengths are present even though you may be unhappy in your marriage at the present time. Yes, even if you are facing what may seem an insurmountable problem, you have the resources within your marriage relationship to overcome that problem. Too often, couples who are experiencing marital problems focus so much on their problems that they overlook the strengths of their relationship. They unwillingly feed their problems. In contrast, couples who are aware of their strengths are not as likely to become discouraged and they use the strengths in their marriage relationship to overcome their problems.

Another wonderful truth is that your marriage relationship can become stronger and more fulfilling. Your marriage can become better regardless of whether it is very happy at the present time or not happy.

One feature of this book that sets it apart from others is that it is not based on opinion. It is based on over 25 years of research with thousands of successful marriages. We have researched the relationships of 6,000 successful marriages from throughout the nation, representing every region of the country and all socioeconomic groups. They came from diverse racial and ethnic backgrounds. They ranged from younger couples to older couples, some married for five years, some for 50 years or more. The average length of marriage was 20 years.

Through this book you have the unique opportunity to learn from successful marriages as these couples share their secrets of success. They will teach us not how marriages fail but how they succeed.

Our research with successful marriages started 25 years ago as part of the larger strong families research which is discussed in the book *Fantastic Families.*[1] The sample of couples covers a time span ranging from 1974 when Nick started the Family Strengths Research Project at Oklahoma State University, continuing through the late 1970's and 1980's at The University of Nebraska where Nick's friend and colleague, Dr. John DeFrain, joined him in a series of national studies and international studies of strong families. The research has continued through the 1990's with Nick at The University of Alabama working with Dr. Donnie Hilliard of Faulkner University to research successful marriages. A total of 6,000 successful couples have been identified.

FAMILY STRENGTHS MODEL

There are six foundational themes that run throughout the marriage relationships of these 6,000 successful couples. They are the same six qualities of strong families which were identified in the pioneer research by Nick Stinnett and John DeFrain. These six qualities that form the foundation for successful marriages are:

1. **Commitment.** Successful couples are dedicated to promoting each other's welfare and happiness. They make their marriage a top priority with respect to how they invest their time and energy.

2. **Appreciation.** These happy couples express a great deal of appreciation to each other. They build each other up psychologically. They give sincere compliments and enhance each other's self-esteem.

3. **Positive Communication.** Husbands and wives who enjoy strong, fulfilling marriage relationships have good communication skills and spend much time talking with each other.

4. **Time Together.** Successful couples spend good quality time with each other and in generous quantities.

5. **Spiritual Well-being.** These happy couples have a strong spir-

itual faith. This spiritual faith gives them strength and purpose.

6. **The Ability to Cope with Stress and Crises.** Successful couples possess good stress management skills and are able to deal with crises in a positive way. They have the ability to see something positive in a bad situation. They are able to view stress or crises as opportunities to grow.

These six qualities are interwoven with every other part of the marriage relationship among these successful couples. You will see them surface throughout this book. They form a common thread, linking together the eight principles which the 6,000 couples have shared as secrets for their marriage success.

THE 10 BEACONS

Look at this book as a celebration of your marriage and a sharing of the 10 principles which can make your marriage voyage successful. The 10 principles shared by the successful couples are:

- Experiencing intimacy
- Enhancing good communication
- Resolving conflict
- Keeping romance in your marriage
- Overcoming chronic stress and hassles
- Navigating dangerous waters
- Weathering the storms of life
- Developing a great sexual relationship
- Nurturing spiritual wellness
- Giving the blessing

These principles work! Your practice of them can bring you more joy and can ensure that your marriage will thrive to your golden wedding anniversary and beyond. Each principle has been confirmed by these 6,000 successful couples. If they can do it, you can do it, regardless of what your marriage is like right now. The successful marriages researched for this book can serve as a lighthouse for your marriage voyage.

Chapter 1

EXPERIENCING INTIMACY

Jean, a Brooklyn resident, paused a moment as her eyes filled with tears before she answered the question of why she and Sid were still happily married after twenty years.

"He is my best friend," she said. "I feel closer to him than anyone."

Jean went on to describe what accounted for this feeling of closeness.

"I can talk with him about anything," Jean continued. "One of the times I felt closest to Sid was early in our marriage when I told him about the time I was sexually molested when I was a little girl.

"This experience was baggage I had carried inside me for a long time," she said. "It had even affected our sexual relationship.

"I poured out my heart and anger to Sid on that evening seventeen years ago," Jean said. "I gave him all the ugly details—things I had never shared with anyone else.

"I cried until no more tears were left. I remember how he held me close and whispered to me over and over that it was all right. He said that it did not have to hurt us all these years later and that I could let it go now."

Sid had reassured her that the sexual assault was not her fault; nor was it her responsibility except that she still carried the bad feelings. He urged her to let those feelings go.

"We talked until the early hours of the morning," said Jean. "I felt as if a great burden had been lifted from my shoulders. I felt closer to Sid at that time than I had ever felt with another human being."

And, of course, there have been many other experiences of closeness in Jean and Sid's marriage. Jean and Sid have experienced something we all long for—intimacy! Such intimacy is closeness between two people enveloped by an atmosphere of deep caring and commitment. Furthermore, there will be many more moments of closeness for Jean and Sid because they have the kind of relationship which generates intimacy.

THE NATURE OF INTIMACY

Would you like to have more intimacy in your relationship? You may certainly experience more special moments of intimacy in your marriage just as surely as the dawn follows night if you understand the nature of intimacy and the principles that foster it.

Intimacy is complete closeness with another. Intimacy means knowing all about your partner in many areas of life. What are his preferences in food, clothes, recreation, and work? What are her dreams and goals for life? What causes his mind to race with creative ideas? What fills her heart with joy (or grief)?

Complete closeness also means sharing many parts of life – working together, playing together. It is being partners, companions, best friends, and lovers. It means having "two hearts that beat as one." Marital intimacy is discovering the essence of yourself through emotional, social, intellectual, and physical union with your partner.

To experience the essence of yourself in your marriage, the environment in the relationship must be right. If we know the nature of that environment, we can be more successful in creating intimacy in the marriage relationship.

THE INTIMACY ENVIRONMENT

Just as a garden needs warm sun and rain to grow, a marriage must have the right kind of conditions in the environment for it to flourish. Four critical principles need to be interwoven into the fabric of the marital environment to nurture intimacy.

TRUST

"My husband has been having an affair for the past year," said Lorraine. "I found out from one of my friends.

"At first, I was in shock. And then I felt like a fool," Lorraine continued. "It means the affair had been going on for about eight months before I knew about it.

"He says that he has ended the affair and that it will not happen again. But I don't really believe him. Obviously, he has lied about other things.

"This has changed a lot about our relationship," said Lorraine. "We don't talk as much as we used to. I don't enjoy being around him.

"Our sexual relationship has certainly been damaged," said Lorraine. "I just don't feel comfortable sharing myself with him emotionally or sexually. The bottom line is that I don't trust him."

Lorraine's example illustrates how a lack of trust spills over into every area of a relationship. When you don't trust someone you feel uncomfortable, a little insecure, and defensive with that person. You are uncertain that this person is for you or will "do right" by you. Therefore, you feel as though you have to be on guard. Unfortunately, just as in Lorraine's marriage, many husbands and wives mistrust each other and are uncertain together. Such conditions make it impossible for true intimacy to develop. The successful couples in our national Marriage Success Research Project indicated that trust is a major characteristic of intimacy and a successful, enduring marriage relationship.

"Jeannette has always been honest with me," said a Midwestern husband. "She doesn't play mind games.

"I know that if I tell anything of a confidential nature she will not repeat it. It means a lot to me that I can depend on her."

A woman living in the Southeast shares, "My husband is one hundred percent for me. I can count on him to be there."

It is easier to trust when there is a reason for doing so. We can more successfully increase the level of trust in marriage by understanding that we will have a higher degree of trust in someone when:

- Trust and confidentiality have not been violated.
- That person's attitudes and actions toward us indicate that he or she is for us and will "do right" by us.
- That person is emotionally supportive of us and is interested in promoting our well-being.
- There is an absence of exploitation or manipulative behavior.
- That person's behavior is honest, sincere, genuine, and consistently real.
- That person expresses acceptance of us rather than rejection.

VALIDATION OR UNCONDITIONAL POSITIVE REGARD

Ed and Tina's marriage of 32 years is one of the happiest and most stable you can imagine. They genuinely enjoy doing many things together and they have a romance in their marriage that would rival that of a newly married couple. We asked them what separated their marriage from so many others.

"I'll tell you one thing that has been important to me is that I have always known that Ed loves me through the bad times as well as the good times," said Tina.

"He loves me even when my behavior is bad and I have acted pretty bad at times," said Tina. "He might not agree with my behavior, but his attitude toward me does not change at all."

Lowell, a husband in Oregon, shares this story.

"A few years ago I lost my job," Lowell said. "Actually I was fired because I had become involved in a conflict situation with my boss.

"I had always had a lot of pride in my work so being fired was not something I had ever considered could happen to me," said Lowell. "My confidence and self-esteem were busted. This was definitely the low point in my career and one of the lowest in my life.

"The main reason I pulled through that difficult time was my wife," said Lowell. "She continued to let me know that she thought I was special and that she had full confidence in me.

"She found me just as attractive and loved me just as much as always even though I was out of a job, depressed, and irritable," said Lowell. "You know that's really something.

"Her unconditional love for me restored my self-confidence and gave me the strength to get through that situation. I tell you, she is quite a woman and I am a lucky man."

There is a priceless beauty and strength in the quality of interaction in Lowell's marriage and in Ed and Tina's marriage. The beauty is that each partner is loved and held in high regard—and that love and high regard do not depend on achievement, status, physical beauty, or being a perfect person!

Each of us longs to be loved by another with a love that does not depend on our performance. It is logical that this is one of our deepest needs. After all, if we are loved conditionally what happens when we no longer achieve as expected? What happens when we lose our physical attractiveness; get older; or lose our political, business, or professional influence and power?

You will feel more secure about your marriage relationship when you know you are loved and esteemed for the person you are and not because of your performance or because of how well you meet a spouse's expectations. The couples in our national Marriage Success Research Project demonstrate that unconditional positive regard and love greatly strengthen a marriage and enhance marital intimacy.

PSYCHOLOGICAL COMFORT

Can you experience intimacy with someone if you are not

comfortable with that person? Many people date and marry someone with whom they do not feel psychologically at ease. They may feel threatened or insecure with the relationship. They may fear that a partner will reject them if they are themselves. So, they go to great lengths to pretend they are something they are not. They continue to play a role and become artificial rather than genuine. In the process, true intimacy is lost.

Perhaps nothing is more important in marital intimacy than the degree to which two people feel psychologically comfortable with each other. A notable characteristic of the successfully married couples in our research is that they are very psychologically comfortable with each other.

"I really like the fact that I can talk with Marty about anything," said a Connecticut wife. "I guess part of it is I know I can trust him. The other is that he is very natural and that makes me feel at ease."

A Texas husband shared, " I think this is a large part of why we feel close to each other. I am so glad my wife does not put on a front, or try to manipulate me."

A Kentucky wife said, "The little acts of considerateness, like giving me a surprise party or helping me do a job that I'm too tired to do are a part of our marriage I would not trade for anything. The fact that he cares for me makes me feel close to him. I never feel that I need to be guarded."

Psychological comfort comes from many unknown sources. However, it is possible to identify some of the characteristics that promote psychological comfort between two people. These include the inclination to:

- See things from your partner's viewpoint (empathy).
- Be natural, have freedom from extreme guardedness.
- Have a helpful attitude (supportiveness)
- Refrain from being judgmental and critical.
- Show respect and consideration.
- Be genuinely interested in your partner.
- Be honest and sincere (do not pretend or put on a front).

- Avoid playing psychological games and trying to manipulate others.
- Be trustworthy and dependable.[1]

COMMITMENT

Liz and Sean are one of the happiest couples we have encountered. They enjoy working and playing together. They talk to each other often about trivial things as well as important issues. Romance is apparent after 18 years of marriage. Their sexual attraction to each other is strong. They genuinely enjoy being together in all aspects of their lives.

Yet, this marriage could easily have ended in divorce. An affair in the fourth year of their marriage almost destroyed the relationship. Sean became involved with a mutual friend with whom he worked. Understandably, she did not remain a mutual friend.

Liz was deeply hurt. She was filled with resentment toward her former friend and toward her husband.

"I can't find the words to describe to you how I felt," said Liz. "I was sick at my stomach and couldn't eat. I lost 20 pounds in four months. I could only sleep two or three hours at a time.

"As you might guess I felt terribly depressed and looked like I was close to death," she said.

"My self-esteem went tumbling down," Liz continued. "I kept thinking I was somehow inadequate. . . that if I had satisfied Sean sexually he would never have become involved with someone else. I resented him for making me feel that way. Maybe hated would be a more accurate word.

"I felt betrayed," Liz shared, "and I no longer trusted Sean."

Another friend of Liz encouraged her to divorce Sean. Her feelings of anger and rejection made Liz very receptive to the suggestion. After all, she wanted to hurt and reject him, too. A lawyer was secured and the process of killing a marriage was speeded up. The final destination of legal termination of the marriage seemed very predictable.

But the predictable did not happen! Liz and Sean did not divorce.

They stayed together and their marriage became stronger than it had ever been. Their happiness and intimacy became greater than they ever imagined.

What made the difference? We turned to Sean to get his story.

"The crucial thing for me was to realize my relationship with Liz was the most important thing. I made the decision that our marriage was top priority for me," said Sean. "I had to make every effort to save it. Even if Liz continued with the divorce, I had to do everything I could to try to save the marriage.

"I ended the affair immediately. This was painful but it was the only thing to do," Sean shared. "I then put all my energy into making the relationship with Liz as good as it could possibly be."

Liz took a different path to reverse the course of marriage destruction she was on. She faced the challenge of overcoming her hurt.

It was not easy. At first, she had turned a deaf ear to Sean's persistent pleas to give him another chance and to start over.

"I was sitting alone late one night looking at the divorce papers," Liz recalled, "And feeling sad about what it meant to end my marriage. I remembered how much in love we had been when we were married.

"For some reason that I still don't understand, I got out old wedding photos. I could still remember our vows we had written and said to each other," she continued. "It came to me that I had promised to love him and stay with him and help him. It was then I decided to keep my promise to Sean.

"I started to forgive Sean that night," she said. "It was not until a good bit later that I was able to completely let go of the hurt. But with the help of God all of the hurt and resentment gradually vanished.

"I guess you could say that the turning point for me was deciding that our marriage was also my top priority – not revenge or making Sean feel guilty for the hurt he had caused me. I am so glad that we both stayed with it through that very tough time."

Sean shared with us "It was a horrible time for us – something I would never want to go through again. But you know we came out of it closer and better than ever. And today we are happier than when we were first married."

Many marriages do not survive an affair. It is one of the most common reasons given for divorce. However, Liz and Sean survived this crisis and came through with a stronger marriage because of their commitment to the marriage and to each other.

Commitment is a powerful force that can help couples overcome great problems and turn stumbling blocks into stepping stones. It can turn tough times into opportunities for growth.

Nothing is more important in building a strong, lasting marriage than commitment. As one wife in Delaware said, "Commitment is loving someone even when they don't act lovable. It is sitting down and listening to someone when you don't feel like listening."

A Florida husband shares, "Commitment is being there for someone, and doing everything you can to promote her happiness and welfare."

An Alabama wife adds, "Commitment is caring that is lasting and no-strings-attached."

They said it in different ways, but a consistent ingredient in all of the happy marriages included in the Marriage Success Research Project was a strong commitment to each other and to the marriage with respect to how they invest their time and energy. An inescapable conclusion from the relationship of these couples is that commitment is a conscious decision one makes to love another.

The presence of a deep commitment creates conditions that make it easier for a couple to trust and to give themselves more completely to each other. Commitment increases intimacy!

Chapter 2

ENHANCING GOOD COMMUNICATION

Communication is the lifeblood of your marriage relationship. You may respect, love, and appreciate your spouse with all your might. However, it is not enough simply to have these feelings. You need to communicate them clearly to your partner.

The nature of your marriage relationship is determined largely by the kind of messages you and your spouse communicate to each other. When a couple slips into a pattern of sending critical, destructive messages to each other, the unfortunate results are often shattered self-esteem and a marriage that neither feels good about. In contrast, if a couple typically sends messages of admiration, affection, and encouragement, the results are that both of them can feel good about themselves and the marriage relationship.

Each of us has a deep need to share thoughts and feelings with another person whom we can trust. We want to be understood. We appreciate the person who gives us the benefit of a doubt or who can overlook the silly or negative things we sometimes say. The nineteenth century English novelist, Dinah Maria Mulock Craik, stated:

"Oh, the comfort, the inexpressible comfort of feeling safe with a person, having neither to weigh thoughts nor to measure words, but pouring them all right out, just as they are, chaff and grain together, certain that a faithful hand will take and sift them, keep what is worth keeping, and with the breath of kindness, blow the rest away."

The type of communication described by Craik is characteristic of the successful couples in our research. They seem to have a keen understanding of each other and they have developed the art of being able to see things from each other's point of view. They are sensitive to each other's feelings. They consistently send positive messages to each other. These couples enjoy good communication because of habits they have nurtured. These habits result in consistent patterns or styles of communication that serve to enrich a marriage relationship. Two important steps in experiencing a more fulfilling marriage relationship are to become aware of the major styles of communication and to adopt a style which will have positive consequences for enhancing your marriage relationship.

STYLES OF COMMUNICATION

We as individuals each have a predominant style of communication – a consistent pattern we use to send messages to other people. Although we do not communicate the same way 100 percent of the time, our communication style is the way we typically communicate. Furthermore, the particular style of communication plays a large role in determining the quality of communication in a marriage relationship.

Becoming more aware of your individual style can be a first step in improving communication with your partner. There are six major styles of communication. As you look at these, remember that not only individuals but also marriages generate a certain style of communication.

- **Silent:** This style tends to be non-communicative. The silent-style person does not initiate conversations easily and has difficulty sharing feelings or thoughts.

- **Game playing:** This style is one of manipulation and exploitation. Dishonesty and deceit are characteristic of this individual's pattern of interacting with others. The game player does not trust others to "do right" by him or her so manipulation is used to make sure the desired results are achieved.

- **Ambiguous:** The communication in the ambiguous style is indirect and unclear. Confusing, obscure, and contradictory messages are typical. This person may simply never have learned to communicate in a clear manner. However, it may also be that he or she has chosen to be ambiguous because of fear of rejection or confrontation. It may be a way to avoid committing to a certain position or a way to avoid responsibility.

- **Destructive:** Here there is a pattern of sending out destructive messages such as criticism and ridicule. The destructive-style communicator often uses sarcasm, "put-downs," or messages that are designed to diminish the self-confidence and self-esteem of others.

- **Open:** This is a pattern of free sharing of one's inner feelings and thoughts. There are no hidden agendas or attempts to manipulate. The communication is direct, honest, and upfront. "What you see is what you get" is characteristic of this communication style and it is easy to trust this person.

- **Constructive:** All of us desire to have others communicate with us in this manner. The constructive style of communication typically involves positive, uplifting messages. There is a consistent pattern of providing messages of encouragement, appreciation, and support.

The game-playing and destructive styles cause the most intense unhappiness and conflict in marriage. It is significant that the most happily married couples – those with strong and lasting marriages – are characterized by open and constructive styles of communication.

COMMUNICATION DIFFERENCES BETWEEN MEN AND WOMEN

The differences between women and men are interesting, amusing, and frustrating to us. Although men and women are more alike than different, the differences are a source of conversation and conflict. This is true of communication, too. While there are more similarities than differences, there are some interesting variations in the ways men and women communicate. There are certain tendencies for each gender.

More men than women engage in certain communication patterns and more women than men use other communication behaviors as the chart below shows.[1]

More Men Than Women:	More Women Than Men:
Engage in the silent style of communication	Engage in the open style, constructive style and destructive style. (Women tend to communicate more – whether positive or negative – than do men)
Express low self-disclosure	Are skilled in starting and maintaining conversations
Use little non-verbal communication (for example, men are less likely to use eye contact to communicate intimacy)	Are skilled in communicating and interpreting non-verbal messages
Focus on facts	Focus on feelings and emotions
Prefer to come to major idea (bottom line) quickly in conversation	Prefer to discuss more elaborately the details and feelings leading up to the major idea in conversation

More Men Than Women:	More Women Than Men:
Communicate distant, impersonal messages	Communicate warm, friendly, attentive messages

When these differences exist in exaggerated form they may cause conflict. Women may become frustrated because their husbands neither express their emotions and feelings nor do they appear interested in learning their wives' feelings.

One important lesson we have learned from couples who have successful, happy marriages is that they make an effort to be sensitive to the communication differences that may exist and attempt to minimize those differences. For example, a husband who is inclined to come to the "bottom line" quickly in a conversation will listen patiently and understandingly to his wife give more details than he may want to hear. And in like manner, his wife, knowing that he does not like too many details, will leave out some of the details and come to the "bottom line" more quickly. This willingness to accommodate each other sends important messages of respect and commitment.

WHAT SHIPWRECKS COMMUNICATION

Couples who are unhappy usually have serious problems in their communication with each other. Certain behaviors are very apt to shipwreck communication.

SARCASM

Sarcasm is one of the biggest communication killers. Although some initially may think of sarcasm as sharp-edged humor or wit, sarcasm is actually veiled anger and hostility. Over a period of time it can make the recipient dread trying to communicate, resulting in more and more avoidance and a gradual drifting apart. Sarcasm also generates resentment and anger in the other partner, causing an acceleration of conflict.

SHADOW TALK

Shadow talk occurs when one partner does not directly let the other know clearly what he or she wants, feels, or expects. Shadow talk is often learned in childhood and is an attempt to test another's feelings about something without risking rejection. Most of us use some shadow talk to protect our feelings. It interferes with clear communication when used so much that definite messages are rarely sent. Instead, the shadow talker hints at or evades the intended message, leaving the other person confused or completely ignorant concerning the real meaning of the message.

Phillip wishes to go to a movie. He shadow talks this to his wife by saying, "A good movie is playing tonight." His wife may think he is simply making conversation.

When she does not respond by saying, "Let's go to the movies," he may feel his request has been rejected. In reality, she never realized it was a request. The request to go to the movies might also be presented as someone else's desire: "Our daughter would like to go to the movies tonight."

OVERGENERALIZATIONS

Overgeneralizations are inaccurate statements which make the other person feel defensive or uncomfortable. Their use can disrupt communication and often lead to conflict. Overgeneralizations often begin, "You always – –" or "You never – –."

"You never remember to get me a gift for my birthday." (He actually forgot her birthday only once out of the six years they have been married.) She may know that she is overgeneralizing; unfortunately if she does this repeatedly she may eventually come to feel that he never gets her a gift for her birthday. He also may know that she is not accurate, but may feel obliged to defend his actions and to explain himself.

INACCURATE ASSUMPTIONS

Much misunderstanding could be avoided if we did not make inaccurate assumptions. For example, Jack loves to play golf and expects his wife to love golf also. When she does not share his enthusiasm, he becomes angry. He is inaccurately assuming that she shares, and should share, his love of golf.

Too often one marriage partner projects personal emotions and desires onto the other without attempting to discover the actual feelings of a mate. For example, a husband, who likes very practical and useful gifts (and assumes his wife does as well) gives his wife a vacuum cleaner as a gift. She actually favors something more personal and responds in anger, "You think I'm a drudge, your servant!" Both are making inaccurate assumptions about the thoughts and feelings of the other and neither has bothered to check the accuracy of those assumptions.

Misunderstandings and conflict also arise when one partner does not communicate feelings and expectations about a certain issue because of the assumption that a partner knows or should know his or her feelings.

Consider the following example from a counseling session:

Wife: He never helps around the house.

Counselor: Have you told him you would like for him to share the housework?

Wife: He knows I need his help and want him to pitch in.

Counselor: But have you communicated this to him?

Wife: Well, no, I haven't.

CULTURAL DIFFERENCES

Couples who come from very different national, racial, socioeconomic, or religious cultures face some obvious barriers to communication. Each partner brings quite different values, attitudes, aspirations, customs, and styles of living.

Vast cultural differences can result in the marriage partners having different frames of reference that can make mutual understanding rather difficult. This is indicated by the fact that marriages in which the spouses are from very different backgrounds (race, religion, ethnicity, socioeconomic status) have a higher divorce rate than do marriages where partners have more similar cultural backgrounds.

Even spouses who have similar cultural backgrounds in every other way may still be very different from each other with respect to the cultures of the families in which the partners grew up. Each person comes from a family that has its own distinct values, customs, traditions, shared common experiences, and manner of communication. For example, some families openly express affection and hug each other a lot. Other families do not openly express affection and may be non-touchers. These different family cultures can sometimes interfere with communication between husband and wife.

Many couples overcome their cultural differences and experience good communication and great marriages. The successful couples in our research have overcome cultural differences by maturity and a willingness to accept and respect their diversity instead of viewing the differences as faults or character flaws. Most of all they conquered their cultural differences by having a strong commitment to each other and to the marriage.

MIND GAMES

Few things shipwreck communication and relationships as effectively as mind games. A mind game or psychological game is interaction between two people that appears to be honest but has a hidden agenda beneath the surface. There is dishonesty and deceit. One person is manipulating the other. The person who plays the mind game plans the interaction to produce a desired effect. People play games because they want to control others, they do not trust others, they fear close relationships, or they do not know better ways of relating to others.

Some mind games are annoying but harmless; others are vicious and destructive. While all of us play psychological games to some extent, an intense and constant use of psychological games may reflect an emotional disturbance in the game player and may cause emotional distress in the victim.

Of the many kinds of psychological games played within a marriage relationship, one of the most destructive is "corner." Clinical research with mentally ill patients suggests that much emotional disturbance is caused when an individual has been continually cornered by a marriage partner or by a parent earlier in life.

The corner game is a process by which one marriage partner interacts with the other in such a way as to place him or her in a situation where anything he or she does is wrong, undesirable or a failure. The game player literally maneuvers the other into a corner so that the victim finds himself or herself in a situation defined as "damned if you do and damned if you don't."

For example, a husband encourages his wife to give parties for his colleagues at work. If she declines, she receives this kind of criticism from her husband:

"Why don't you give parties like my friends' wives do? You're the only one who doesn't. You are hurting my chances of climbing in the company. Doesn't it matter to you?"

However, if she does give parties, he criticizes:

"The roast beef was awful. Why didn't you talk more with Mrs. Anderson tonight? I don't see why you couldn't have done a better job of circulating among the guests. You're not friendly."

Another common mind game is the "It is your decision" game, where one spouse escapes the responsibility of making a decision by placing the burden of the choice completely upon the shoulders of the other partner. Such comments as these are often made:

"It makes no difference to me."

"Whatever you would like to do is fine with me."

"But honey, you know so much more about this than I do. You make the decision."

By responding this way the game player escapes the responsibility of facing any consequences. If it turns out to be wrong, it was, after all, the victim who made the decision.

When husbands and wives play this game with each other about their children, it can become especially destructive. A husband, for example, may refuse to help his wife make decisions concerned with rearing their children. Then, when something goes wrong, or one of the children gets into some kind of trouble, the husband self-righteously blasts his wife with a charge of "You're not rearing our children right."

Playing mind games is likely to drive husbands and wives apart. Use of mind games prevents mutual understanding and leads to confused, inaccurate communication. Furthermore, the deceit involved destroys intimacy; spouses must be able to trust one another for full intimacy to be possible.

INTIMIDATION

Another common way that husbands and wives destroy their communication with each other is intimidation. We can intimidate each other in many ways – throwing a temper tantrum, engaging in actual physical abuse, ridiculing, threatening to leave, or becoming very cold and sullen.

Jan and Scott are in the midst of a heated argument – one of many they have been experiencing. This time the conflict is over how they will spend some extra money they have. She wants a new dining room table while he wants a nice set of tools that will help him to work on the car. Jan quickly begins to yell at Scott that he doesn't treat her right. He doesn't love her. She threatens to take the children and leave him. Scott gives in and agrees to buy the table.

Even though a spouse may get his or her way by intimidating the other, it is a losing strategy in the long run. Intimidation is self-defeating because it creates resentment in the other partner. That spouse may withdraw and avoid communication or react with hostility and even resort to intimidation tactics. Over a period of time communication deteriorates and the relationship becomes less satisfying.

An important characteristic of couples with successful marriages is that they do very little intimidation of each other. In contrast, distressed couples are more likely to engage in intimidation behavior a great deal. Happy couples with lasting marriages minimize behavior that is confronting or threatening. As a result, these couples create a marriage relationship that is secure and positive.

SENDING CONTRADICTORY MESSAGES

"How would you like to go camping this weekend?" he asks with an excited expression on his face. "The forecast is for great weather. It will be fun."

"Yes, that would be good," she replies. However, her facial expression is one of boredom and slight irritation.

He is confused. She is sending two conflicting messages. Her words say, "Yes." Her body language says, "No." Which does she mean? Contradictory communication is confusing and requires an extra effort to be understood and interpreted.

MAKING COMMUNICATION FLOURISH

COMMITMENT

"I can tell you the one ingredient which has been most important in our marriage from my point of view is that I know Tim is always there for me," said Betty. "I know he has my best interests at heart.

"I can count on him and I trust him completely," she shared. "I feel comfortable talking with him about anything. He is my number one confidant."

Communication can flourish in a relationship filled with mutual appreciation, trust, respect, and understanding. In such a relationship both spouses feel the freedom and safety to share their innermost feelings and thoughts with each other.

Upon what foundation is such a relationship based? To a large extent it grows from the presence of one quality – a strong commitment to promote the welfare and happiness of each other. Each spouse knows that the other will do everything possible to create and maintain the conditions in which the potential and well-being of each one are best realized.

When partners have this positive commitment from each other, they have more trust and are more likely to have relaxed, open, and attentive communication. This type of communication in turn contributes to a higher degree of marriage happiness.

DEVELOP COMMON INTERESTS

"From the beginning, Jenny and I have been heavily involved in our careers," said Ted. "It has been a challenge to balance work and family, but I think we have done a pretty good job of not letting the pressures of our jobs reduce the quality of our marriage relationship.

"One reason is that there are similarities in our two careers," he continued. "And we talk a lot about our respective job challenges. We enjoy that communication.

"Discussing different aspects of our jobs with each other really helps to reduce work stress for both of us. We also get good ideas from each other that we can take back to our jobs."

Not all couples find their jobs to be a particularly enjoyable center point for communication. Other common interests need to be cultivated and hobbies are one arena from which many couples generate common interests.

"I discovered after five years of marriage that Ernest had his hobbies, and I had my hobbies, but we really had none we enjoyed together," said Sue. "This meant we were spending more and more of our leisure time separately."

Sue decided that while it was good that they had hobbies they enjoyed separately, they also needed to have something they could enjoy doing together. Otherwise, she was concerned their communication would gradually diminish. So she took action.

"My hobbies for the most part deal with clothing design and sewing, and I did not think Ernest would develop an interest in those things," she laughed. Sue made the commitment to develop an interest in some of Ernest's hobbies and to get involved in them.

"Ernest loves to fly and do scuba diving. I began taking flying lessons and did get my pilot's license. We enjoy flying together and we fly often. It is also safer when we fly now since we are both pilots.

"It was harder for me to get into scuba diving," Sue said, "because I never liked to get my face in the water. It would give me a panic reaction.

"But then our son wanted to scuba dive, too, so I thought the whole family could do this together," she said. "I literally forced myself to take lessons. Gradually I got to where I could go underwater without being terrified.

"I stayed with it and passed the test. I was so proud of myself when I received the scuba diving certificate. It took a lot of courage. But I am so glad I did it because this is something my husband, my son, and I enjoy doing together."

Cultivating common interests, such as Sue did, gives couples something to talk about and do together that is enjoyable. It generates positive communication. It is a means of forming closer bonds.

LISTEN

Frustrated at her husband's chronic failure to listen, a wife tried an experiment one evening at the dinner table. She passed the chicken to her husband and asked him if he would like to try her new recipe – fried chicken breaded with arsenic. He ate with gusto and agreed that the chicken was delicious.

Listening is a vital part of communication, but too often we are more interested in talking or with our own concerns than we are with listening. Listening is a neglected part of communication skills. Marriage counselors commonly hear such complaints as, "Talking to my husband is like talking to a brick wall," or "My wife is so wrapped up in herself that she never listens to me."

Listening is essential to good communication and to successful marriage relationships because listening helps us gain important information about each other and about what is going on in our lives. But the biggest benefit of listening is that when we genuinely listen to someone we send a very important message – respect. Our listening says to the other person, "I respect you enough to listen. I am interested in you and want to hear what you have to say."

This one behavior is very closely interwoven with marriage happiness. A marriage partner who does not listen causes the other to feel neglected and unimportant. This makes it much more likely that dissatisfaction and misery will grow in the relationship.

Couples with a high degree of marriage happiness are good listeners. They are wholistic listeners. They listen to each other's words. But they do more than listen to each other's words. They also listen to each other's feelings.

"When I talk about something that concerns me, it is usually the feeling I have about the issue that matters most to me," Angela said. "I guess the words I use are just a way of trying to share those feelings.

"Sometimes my words don't do a very good job of expressing my feelings," she continued. "One thing that is priceless about Paul is that he hears my emotions. He often knows my thoughts and feelings even when they have not been communicated very well by my words."

Wholistic listening also involves the ability to put yourself in your mate's situation and to view the world as he or she is seeing it. Persons who do this can better understand where a spouse is coming from. Persons who are wholistic listeners are sensitive to both non-verbal behavior and voice tone.

Ray, for example, can tell when his wife is tense because she speaks more rapidly and in a higher pitch. One of his cues that she is tired is that her voice becomes monotone and she speaks more slowly.

Couples who are sensitive to each other's voice tone and non-verbal behavior not only experience better, more accurate communication but they also have a higher degree of marriage satisfaction. Distressed couples, in contrast, are less sensitive to each other's non-verbal behavior and less accurate in interpreting non-verbal cues.

Nothing is more important to good communication than listening. To a large extent, being a good listener is a reflection of commitment – commitment to take the time to listen, commitment to listen sometimes when we don't feel like it, and commitment to give a partner undivided attention.

CHECK THE MEANING OF COMMUNICATION

In the classified ad section of a small-town newspaper, the following ads appeared:

On Monday – FOR SALE: R.D. Jones has one sewing machine for sale. Phone 958 after 7 p.m. and ask for Mrs. Kelly who lives with him cheap.

On Tuesday – NOTICE: We regret having erred in R.D. Jones' ad yesterday. It should have read: One sewing machine for sale. Cheap. Phone 958 and ask for Mrs. Kelly who lives with him after 7 p.m.

On Wednesday – R.D. Jones has informed us that he has received several annoying telephone calls because of the error we made in his classified ad yesterday. His ad stands corrected as follows: R.D. Jones has one sewing machine for sale. Cheap. Phone 958 after 7 p.m. and ask for Mrs. Kelly who loves with him.

On Thursday – NOTICE: I, R.D. Jones, have no sewing machine for sale; I smashed it. Don't call 958 as the telephone has been taken out. I have not been carrying on with Mrs. Kelly. Until yesterday she was my housekeeper, but she quit.[2]

Inaccurate interpretations of messages happen very easily and cause unnecessary misunderstanding and conflict. One key to good communication among happily married couples is the ability to check the meaning of messages that are not clear. Meanings can be clarified by questions or comments such as "I'm not sure what you mean," or "This is my understanding of what you said. Tell me if this is accurate."

Giving this type of feedback reduces the possibility of misunderstanding and tends to develop more attentive listening. It provides a method of confirming whether the message you heard is the message your spouse intended.

As with all types of interpersonal responses, feedback is more effective if it is not overused. Care should be taken that the phrasing of the feedback does not sound artificial and insincere. Avoid "parroting" a spouse's message back. Instead try to paraphrase it.

TAKE TIME

Just as flowers must have rain and sunlight to grow, communication must have an environment which is conducive for it to take place. An essential part of that environment is time. There must be time to gather our thoughts and express them. There must be someone who will take the time to listen. The high stress, hurried nature of our society does not provide an environment filled with time for marriage relationships. Couples must create that type of environment for themselves.

One of the major problems for marriages today is that couples do not spend enough time together. They are fragmented by the demands of work, community, and separate leisure-time activities. The situation in many marriages today is that one or both partners must work at two jobs just to provide basic necessities.

While many couples are successful at balancing the demands of work, community and home, the experience for some couples is that they spend so little time together that their ability to communicate deteriorates. Husbands and wives are often unaware of what is going on in the hearts and minds of each other because they simply are not with each other enough to know. These marriages become disconnected and fail to develop identity and unity. It is no surprise that those in unhappy marriages spend much less time in communication than do happily married couples.

The happily married couples in our Marriage Success Research Project spend a lot of time communicating with each other and they take steps to make the time for communication.

Toni and Sal have a relationship in which they do many things together. "We eat dinner together every night," Toni shared. "We do household chores together, and we have a date night once a week."

When Carrie and Joe found themselves drifting into a pattern of spending less and less time in communication, they took steps to change it.

"We were always rushed," said Joe. "We were often not home together in the evenings. When we were together, we were preoccupied with other things. There seemed to be no time when we could just sit down and talk with each other in a relaxed manner.

"Part of the problem was we were involved in too many things," Joe said. "We were overextended."

"The first thing we did was to take a look at everything we were involved in and how much those involvements were demanding our time," said Carrie. "We were shocked when we put it on paper. No wonder we were not spending time together!

"The next step we took was to go through the list and ask, 'Is this activity necessary?' 'Does it make us happy?' 'Is this more important than our marriage?'

"The surprising thing to us was how many of those involvements received an answer of 'No' from both of us on all three questions," said Carrie. "We eliminated those activities. Letting those things go gave us more time together and also got rid of an unbelievable amount of stress.

"The third step we took was to do more fun activities together," Carrie continued. "We both enjoy canoeing so we often canoe in nice weather. We also make a point of scheduling more time together each day.

"For example, we take a walk together every evening," Carrie shared. "Sometimes on our walks by the lake near our home we can see beavers swimming or hear them slap their tails on the water. We look forward to that. We find these walks are a great time for talking because there are no distractions. There are no telephone calls, no television, and no chores staring us in the face. We can just concentrate on each other."

This three-step process described by Carrie and Joe is typical of the way that couples with strong, lasting marriages create time for meaningful communication. This type of effort nurtures better communication and also a higher degree of marriage satisfaction.

KEEP IT POSITIVE

Marie is irritated at Chuck because he did not get all the clothes washed as he had promised he would do while she was at a community agency board meeting most of the evening. "You just lied to me," she explodes. "It's disgusting that you can't keep your word. Now we don't have anything decent to wear tomorrow."

Chuck tries to explain that he had a lengthy call from his boss about a problem at work. "You just didn't want to do it!" she charges. "You want me to do everything."

"Well, you certainly don't do everything," he hotly replies. "I cooked dinner last night. I've been doing a lot of that lately. You can't cook a decent meal even when you try – which isn't often."

This is a typical pattern for Marie and Chuck. The last few years have seen them become increasingly more negative in their communication. They exchange criticism and put-downs; they complain. Conversations are centered on unpleasant events and on what they don't like. Sadly but understandably, Marie and Chuck are feeling less positive about themselves, each other, and their relationship.

Like Marie and Chuck, many couples fall into the trap of engaging primarily in negative communication. Some of these couples would be shocked to discover that a high percentage of their communication is negative: complaints, criticism, put-downs, griping, accusations, and blaming. This type of communication makes it difficult to feel good about the relationship. It is self-defeating if the couple really want to have a satisfying marriage.

Couples who have a negative pattern of communication do not have to continue in that mode. They can change. The change will come by developing new habits of interaction, modeled from what we know about the communication patterns of successful marriages. In contrast to distressed couples, happily married couples do the following:

- More often express appreciation, respect and validation of each other.
- Much more often engage in positive – rather than negative,

communication; they are less likely to escalate conflict and more likely to talk about pleasant events.

- Less often exchange complaints and criticisms.

Happy couples establish a pattern of giving each other positive feedback. They come to accept these positive assessments as accurate and integrate them into their self-perceptions and their views about marriage. This, in turn, propels them to an even greater degree of positive interaction. Of course, the outcome is that their motivation to nurture a successful, caring relationship is increased.

Chapter 3

RESOLVING CONFLICT

" **A** nd they lived happily ever after." That's the way all the fairy tales ended. Maybe that explains the widely held belief that couples with good marriages have no conflict. Naturally, too, a couple with this belief who find themselves in conflict may fear that their marriage is a failure or in danger.

Conflict occurs in every relationship – particularly in intimate relationships such as marriage. Happy couples experience conflict. They get irritated at each other; they quarrel. But unlike many distressed couples they make positive, constructive use of conflict. Happy couples do not allow their conflict to become a war. They minimize destructive anger and, rather than trying to tear each other down, they keep their focus on how best to solve the problem.

One of the most important principles we have learned from our research with couples who have happy, lasting marriages is that couples can make positive, creative use of conflict. We can learn to react and respond in ways that deal effectively with anger. Disagreement can be expressed without destructive hostility. Successful resolutions to conflict can be reached.

WHY CONFLICT HAPPENS

There are endless specific reasons for why conflict occurs. However, certain major reasons contribute to most of the marital conflicts that couples experience.

INTIMACY

Although it sounds contradictory, the most basic reason for marital conflict is the intimacy involved in the marriage relationship. Most of us feel more free to disagree with those persons who are closest to us. It may not be "safe" to disagree with your boss, for example. In any close relationship such as marriage, there are also more opportunities for conflict regardless of how satisfying the relationship may be, simply because the couple spends so much time together and because they share so many aspects of their lives.

BASIC DIFFERENCES

Spouses often have conflict because of the basic differences between them. They may have very different temperaments and personalities; their goals may be incompatible. Different religious, racial, ethnic, socioeconomic, or cultural backgrounds can create ample opportunity for misunderstanding and feelings of rejection – especially if spouses are not able to accept and respect such differences in each other.

Much conflict can also arise when the husband and wife come from very different family cultures. For example, a frequent source of conflict for Robert and Elaine has been behavior at dinner. Elaine was reared in a family where dinner was an occasion for visiting and talking about whatever was of concern to family members. A major purpose of dinner was fellowship. Robert, in contrast, came from a family that ate quickly and mostly in silence. The main purpose of dinner was to eat, after which family members got up and left. It was not an occasion for visiting. The family cultures of Robert and Elaine clashed on this issue. Elaine was disappointed and hurt over Robert's silent rush through dinner. Robert was irritated at Elaine's insistence on talking and lingering while he was trying to eat. When they became aware of their different family upbringing in this respect, they were able to understand the reason behind their disagreement. A little tolerance and consideration cleared up the problem.

TRYING TO MAKE A PARTNER OVER

Often when we discover a characteristic we don't like in a spouse we try to get him or her to change. Sometimes people marry with the intention of remodeling a partner. They may try to change a partner's values, attitudes, likes, dislikes, interests, or certain personality characteristics. The result is usually conflict and resentment.

Each of us is likely to resist being changed by another, especially when it is against our wishes. When one partner tries to change another, it implies displeasure with that partner as a person. Feelings of rejection and resentment are common in the spouse who is the object of the attempted change. Although suggestions within moderation can be helpful and beneficial, persistent requests for change can develop into nagging and even pointed attacks. Finally, open conflict can break out with both spouses attacking and retaliating.

POWER STRUGGLES AND COMPETITION

Power struggles within the relationship are responsible for some of the most intense and destructive marital conflict. Husband and wife are in a continual struggle when everything is a win-lose situation. Such struggle greatly increases their sense of threat and uncertainty in the marriage and marital happiness is greatly reduced.

Loyd and Frances both have strong power needs. Their relationship has become a contest to determine who exercises the most power. "We have a lot of fights," said Loyd. "You know, in a way, I think we both want the conflict. It's just a part of the game to see who wins out." Both Loyd and Frances try to enhance their feelings of self-worth and competency by dominating the other.

In our society people are expected to compete, both in school and in the world of work. It is not surprising that this competitive spirit sometimes carries over into marriage.

Donald and Linda continually compare themselves in terms of their salaries, promotions, prestige, community activities, and even number of friends. Instead of sharing the joy of Linda's accomplishment when she receives a promotion, Donald feels "beaten" and resentful. Rather than being supportive of Donald's volunteer efforts, Linda diminishes his achievements. They often belittle or ignore each other's successes and good fortunes.

A competitive marriage relationship becomes too much like the business world with a ruthless drive for success and recognition. When extreme competitiveness characterizes a marriage, both husband and wife find that emotional security in each other is reduced or lost.

TREMENDOUS TRIFLES

Slurping coffee, leaving the cap off of the toothpaste tube, dirty clothes left on the floor, mumbling, nervous mannerisms, jingling coins or car keys in the pocket, and irritating verbal expressions – these are examples of tremendous trifles. They are petty irritants that can add up and cause serious conflict. They may damage the marriage relationship if they are not dealt with effectively.

Spouses may feel that these trifles are too insignificant to mention. But eventually they become so annoyed by the trifles that they express their irritation openly.

"I get so irked at Chris because he says, 'You know' all the time. He tacks it on everything; it makes me want to scream," said Susan. "But when I say anything about it I feel petty and tacky. That makes me more angry."

These tremendous trifles are most damaging to a relationship when they are kept inside and resentment is allowed to build up over a period of time. They are most likely to be kept in perspective when they are realized for what they are – trifles. Successful couples prevent trifles from gaining undue importance by discussing them as soon as they begin to be irritants.

DIFFERENT ROLE EXPECTATIONS

We all bring certain role expectations with us to marriage. For example, you have definite expectations of yourself, your marriage partner, and your marriage. Sometimes the two people in the marriage have expectations that contrast sharply.

Herb grew up with a mother who was a full-time homemaker. The entire family appreciated the fact that she could devote her energies to the care of the home and family. Furthermore, she enjoyed cooking and baking. Preparing a meal was an act of love from her perspective.

Herb valued these roles that his mother had assumed. His wife, Joan, grew up in a family where her mother had a career and actually earned a higher income than did her father. She did not cook often; and she didn't really enjoy it. Joan identified strongly with her mother and planned from an early age to have a career as a veterinarian. Joan also had little interest in cooking and never learned how to do much cooking. Yet Herb expected her to be a full-time homemaker. Not only did he expect her to prepare the same kind of wonderful meals that his mother had fixed, but he expected Joan to take the same pleasure in cooking as his mother. Not surprisingly their expectations clashed and resulted in considerable conflict.

Happy couples are proficient at realizing when a particular conflict is due to role expectations that do not match. They avoid blaming the conflict on each other's "bad" qualities. They also are good at talking through their expectations so that they understand each other better. They also are more willing to be adaptable and to modify their behavior or expectations.

PRINCIPLES FOR RESOLVING CONFLICT SUCCESSFULLY

Couples who have happy and successful marriages have learned some principles or techniques that help them to resolve their conflict. These principles really work and are not complicated. If you incorporate these principles into your relationship, you will notice a significant improvement in how you resolve conflict.

BE ADAPTABLE

How could Herb and Joan resolve their conflict of expectations? Herb could change his expectations and accept Joan pursuing a career. Since she is not interested in cooking, he could prepare their meals or they could eat out most of the time. On the other hand, Joan could change her expectations and be a full-time homemaker. She could learn to cook and develop an appreciation for that role. Or they might compromise. Herb and Joan could share the cooking duties. Joan might work part-time. The important idea is that Herb and Joan need not allow their clash of expectations to destroy their marriage. There are many ways that they can resolve their problem.

Adaptability is the willingness of an individual to modify his or her own behavior. It is a prominent quality among couples with happy, lasting marriages.

The evidence from numerous research studies suggests that happy couples are more willing to modify their behavior than are unhappy couples. Happy couples use mutual "give and take" much more as a way of dealing with disagreement than do couples who divorce. Couples who resolve conflict most effectively and constructively view each other as being more cooperative than do those couples who respond to conflict in a destructive manner.

Leroy and Margie are on their first camping trip in the mountains. Leroy is enjoying the experience, but Margie is not. She does not like "roughing it." Also, the mountain air is cooler than she expected and she is uncomfortable.

Sensing this, Leroy says, "Let's go. You're cold and not having a good time. We can do something else that we will both enjoy."

Margie replies, "But you are enjoying this very much. We'll stay and it'll probably get better. We can buy a jacket for me tomorrow and I'll be more comfortable."

Both Leroy and Margie are willing to be adaptable and to cooperate with each other. The important outcome of this expression of adaptability is that it transforms conflict from a clash of wills to a courtesy contest. Another important result is that Leroy perceives that Margie wants to please him and Margie perceives that Leroy wants to please her. This willingness and desire to support each other is appreciated regardless of which solution is selected. Adaptability, the willingness to change your behavior for the well being and happiness of your partner, communicates respect and consideration.

DON'T AVOID CONFLICT

Many people believe that a good marriage is one in which there is no disagreement. They think that open conflict implies disharmony and that they have somehow failed in their marriage. Consequently, they repress their feelings of dissatisfaction and aggression. They keep their conflict underground and it does not get resolved. As a result, tension, resentment, and anger continue to grow because the underlying dissatisfaction has not been eliminated.

There are numerous ways people choose to avoid conflict. One is by simply being unresponsive to the concerns or frustrations of another person.

Bernard and Lana are sitting in the living room. A nice fire is burning in the fireplace. A fire is also burning in Lana. She is hot because they have just received an overdraft notice from the bank. She is expressing her agitation to Bernard. Lana is asking how this happened and why Bernard purchased a $400 shotgun this month. She wants Bernard to help her think through how they are going to deal with the facts: they are $500 overdrawn at the bank and there are 10 more days left until payday.

Yet, Bernard says little. In fact, Bernard is not even looking at Lana; he continues to read the newspaper. When he does say anything it is a passive "Hmm" or "Well, I don't know."

Bernard's lack of responsiveness makes Lana more angry. Her voice grows louder. The large, hard-covered novel she has been holding in her lap suddenly goes flying through the air, crashing through the newspaper Bernard has been holding up as if to shield his face from hers. The large book lands with a thud squarely on his face. Bernard, his face somewhat red from the impact, is now for the first time looking directly into the eyes of Lana. Also, for the first time, they are both engaged in a discussion – a loud one at first, but at least a two-way conversation. Bernard has finally become responsive. Hopefully, he can be responsive in the future without the jolt of a large book!

Humor can be a wonderful way to reduce tension in a conflict situation. But it can be misused and become dysfunctional if it is used to avoid conflict.

"He doesn't like to argue," Bettina said. "So when I am upset about something and I try to talk about it, he will just crack one joke after another. I can't get him to be serious enough to discuss it with me. It is infuriating."

Sometimes conflict is avoided by changing the subject or walking away when disagreement begins. Intimidating a partner by threatening to leave the relationship is a strategy some use to get their way and avoid conflict at the same time.

Couples with happy, lasting marriages do not avoid conflict. They deal with it directly; they communicate. They are responsive. Happily married couples more often discuss conflict situations while unhappy couples tend to avoid dealing with the issue. By confronting the conflict directly, successful couples more often solve the problem and get rid of their resentment and hostility.

DON'T GET CAUGHT IN A CYCLE OF CONFLICT

Successful couples do not allow themselves to get caught in a cycle of conflict. They do not focus all their energies and time on the conflict but rather they direct their energies toward solving the problem.

Many couples experience unnecessary misery in their relationship because they focus on the conflict itself rather than the issue involved. Their interaction deteriorates into a competitive game of wits where victory means the enhancing of one person's ego by belittling the other.

The objective in this pattern is not to solve the problem or to gain insight into the issue but instead to attack the person who takes a different viewpoint. Attacks lead to counterattacks. Each partner becomes hypnotized by his or her virtues and the mate's faults. The real issues get lost in the battle and any true conflict resolution or problem solving is prevented.

There are some major behaviors which are typical of the conflict – centered pattern. They are as follows:

Accusations
Blaming
Making threats
Hostile questions
Put-downs
Name-calling
Sarcasm

These types of behavior erect barriers which make it difficult to resolve conflict or solve a problem successfully.[1] In a happy, lasting marriage each person is willing to assume responsibility for his or her behavior and takes steps to eliminate or minimize these types of behavior listed above. As a result, they are effective in resolving the real issue and feel more positive about their relationship.

DON'T GUNNYSACK

A gunnysack is a big burlap sack used extensively by farmers and shipping companies. Gunnysacks are strong and deep. They can be filled with an incredible amount of produce or other material.

We often gunnysack with our emotional baggage. We carry that heavy bag around wherever we go, filled with resentments, hurts, grievances, and anger at the wrongs we have suffered at the hands of others. At strategic times (usually in the heat of conflict) we reach deep into the gunnysack and pull out one or more grievances and, with a vengeance, throw them at the person with whom we are having conflict.

Jason would like to buy a new sports car – a Mustang convertible – that he has wanted for a long time. Jenn thinks their old Toyota is just fine and that spending this much money on a new car that they don't really need is a foolish use of their limited financial resources. She strongly believes they should use what little extra money they have to buy a new washing machine and dryer since their old ones have had to be repaired several times.

Jason becomes very frustrated and gets into a shouting match with Jenn. He accuses her of not loving him. To reinforce his accusation he reaches into his gunnysack and hurls out the fact that she only gave him a "cheap" tie for his last birthday. When Jenn tries to explain that they were overdrawn at the bank that month, Jason reaches into his gunnysack again and pulls out another grievance.

This grievance is that during the Christmas holidays of the past year, at her insistence, they spent more time visiting with her parents than with his mother. Before Jenn could even respond to that complaint, Jason reached into the gunnysack again and hurled yet another accusation – that Jenn has never liked his mother!

How could Jenn respond to this gunnysacking? She really can't because she has been overwhelmed with three or four grievances at once. But in this case Jason is not interested in solving any of those complaints. He is using them to intimidate Jenn. He wants to make her feel guilty so that she will be agreeable to purchasing the sports car.

This way of dealing with conflict is charged with negative emotions. Over a period of time Jason's repeated use of gunnysacking will cause resentment and may influence Jenn to engage in similar tactics. It will certainly increase their level of marriage dissatisfaction and will be counterproductive in settling their disagreements.

Happy couples are much less likely to use gunnysacking than are distressed couples. Instead, they resolve their grievances as they emerge rather than storing them in a gunnysack to be used later.

DON'T BE PASSIVE-AGGRESSIVE

One of the most difficult conflict patterns to deal with is passive-aggressive behavior. The goal of persons who use this strategy is to act aggressively but in an indirect way so that they do not have to accept responsibility for their hostility. They manipulate the situation so that they can deny any aggressive intention. They may smile pleasantly and give a superficial appearance of being agreeable and cooperative while planning an aggressive, hostile act or trap. Anger and low self-esteem are behind the behavior. Passive-aggressive persons feel unsafe in dealing with conflict in an open, direct way so they use this indirect strategy.

Jean must attend a PTA meeting tonight. She asks Gary if he will please load the dishwasher and also wash, dry, and put up a load of the baby's clothes while she is attending the meeting.

Gary does not wish to do this, but he smiles and says, "Yes, dear, I will be glad to do that. You go on to the meeting and have a good time. I will take care of everything here."

When Jean returns home from the meeting, she finds three plates have been "accidentally" broken. She also finds washing powder "accidentally" spilled on the floor and some of the baby's clothes have been dropped on the way from the dryer to the bedroom.

Do you think Jean will ask Gary to help out in this way again? Gary is hopeful that his behavior will discourage her from future requests of this type.

Although he appeared to be pleasant and cooperative, his underlying anger and hostility led him to sabotage his "helpful" behavior. If Jean confronts him about this, he replies, "I'm sorry, Jean. It was just an accident. I was trying to help after all."

Happy couples with lasting marriages do not engage in passive-aggressive behavior. They are direct and open in dealing with their conflict because they feel safe and comfortable with each other.

STAY OFF THE CONFLICT ESCALATOR

"What usually seems to happen with us," shares Katie, "is that we have a disagreement. It starts off with something mild and then one or both of us get mad. The whole thing kicks up to another step. We say really mean, ugly things to each other. It's like we see who can hurt the most. Sometimes we end up in a physical fight. Last week he hit me and threw me into the table. I had to go to the emergency room. As you can see, I'm still wearing the knee brace."

Many couples allow themselves to get on an escalator of conflict and quickly become increasingly more destructive as they move further away from resolving the issue. Five levels of conflict are identified by the Levels of Marital Conflict Model.[2] This model was originated by a conflict management consultant and was later adapted for application in marital therapy by a social-work educator and practitioner.

It is helpful to understand each of these five levels of conflict because each level has different objectives, negotiation styles, and emotional climates. As a couple moves from the first level to the fifth level, the conflict becomes more destructive, the behavior grows more irrational, the issues get more confused, and the goal of trying to solve the problem becomes less and less the objective of the couple.

Couples who are successful at getting off of this conflict escalator take a very crucial step. When they find themselves in an intense, destructive level they de-escalate the conflict level to one in which resolutions are easier.

The five levels of conflict are: (I) problems to solve, (II) disagreements, (III) contest, (IV) fight or flight, and (V) war. The **war** level is the most destructive and the **problems to solve** level is the level at which couples are most likely to resolve their differences in a positive way.

Level I: Problems to Solve

Successful couples keep their level of conflict focused on solving the problem. This has positive consequences for their marriages because conflict at this level is not over issues that threaten the relationship. The concern at this level is resolving different viewpoints. The issue may be not so serious, such as where to vacation, or very serious, such as whether or not to have children.

Regardless of how serious the issue may be, the major objective of a couple at this level of conflict is to solve the problem to everyone's benefit. They do not aim to hurt each other or win a contest or protect themselves. Their negotiation style is open, direct, and clear. The emotional climate at this level is one of hope because the couple are confident they can solve the problem.

Level II: Disagreements

Couples who have escalated to this level of conflict perceive their conflict as centering on their relationship rather than a specific problem. Their conflicts are motivated by a need to defend themselves more than by the need to solve a problem. So their major objective is self-protection.

The emotional climate at this level of conflict is one of uncertainty. Their trust in each other is lowered. Because they are unsure of how much support they can count on receiving from each other they become defensive in their communication. They become cautious about showing their feelings and they begin to be guarded in their interaction.

Level III: Contest Level

When the conflict accelerates to this level, the major objective becomes even further removed from solving the problem. The objective here is winning. The conflict issues have accumulated and are difficult to disentangle at this level. Hope has diminished and frustration grows.

The couple perceive that there are not enough resources to go around and an attitude of "I'm looking out for me" emerges. Strong competitiveness, blaming, and accusations begin to dominate the relationship. Psychological game playing and manipulations are common at this level.

Level IV: Fight or Flight Level

The couple who escalate to this level of conflict have moved far from any intention of trying to solve the problem. The major objective here is to hurt the other person. There are feelings of "My partner cannot change or will not change" and "I am not the one who needs to change."

Feelings of alienation and antagonism are typical of this level. The partners are becoming more unhappy and perceive that their relationship is satisfying fewer of their needs. One or both partners may bring others into the conflict, not to support the marriage or help solve the problem, but as a judge to say one partner is right and the other is wrong.

Couples who stay in this level and continue their marriage may exclude each other more and more. They may stop eating or talking together and forget anniversaries. They may attempt to hurt each other through put-downs, blaming, rejection, or sometimes by becoming involved in an affair. Couples who decide to end their relationship in this level are often involved in hostile divorce proceedings.

Level V: War Level

The conflict between a couple is focused on each other's personalities at this level. The objective is not just to hurt but to destroy each other. They have no hope for the relationship; they do not believe they can resolve their differences. They often perceive the costs of leaving the relationship to be greater than the costs of staying. So, in a sense, they may come to believe that the only way to escape the relationship is by destroying each other.

The perceptions of the partners become distorted and irrationality is high. Partners at this level are strongly inclined toward revenge behavior. Compulsive behavior, such as stalking, often emerges. Partners increasingly use force to accomplish their aims and violence is common.

DEVELOP A GOOD PROBLEM-SOLVING FORMULA

Couples who successfully resolve conflict develop an effective formula for solving the problem. There are certain key elements in this formula.

Respect Disagreement

This one quality does so much to minimize anger and frustration. Because they accept and respect each other's right to disagree, they don't feel as threatened and defensive. This, in turn, reduces the need for power struggles and manipulation.

Identify the Problem

It is very helpful when a person takes the time to think through what is really bothering him or her before bringing it up to a spouse. Couples can spend large amounts of time quarreling about symptoms without ever touching on the underlying problem. For example, it is not uncommon for couples to spend several sessions with a marriage counselor before they identify what their real problem is.

A wife in New York shares an effective strategy that she and her husband have used to clarify problems.

"I write down what is bothering me," she said. "Then I write down why it is a problem to me. I also list specific things my husband could do to help solve the problem.

"He does the same thing when there is something really bugging him," she added. "This is simple but we have found it to be very helpful."

Express Feelings

Conflict involves emotion and we are emotional beings. Each of us wishes to maximize positive emotions and minimize negative emotions. Therefore it is important for a couple to share their emotions in a conflict situation. This should not be done in a destructive manner but in a constructive, informative manner. It can be therapeutic to know that your spouse has really listened and understands you. Also, it is helpful when you know how your partner feels about an issue, because then you are in a better position to help solve the problem.

In many marriage conflicts, emotions explode in accusations and yelling: "You're just a jerk!" "You're so stubborn!"

These kinds of accusations and labels make the recipient feel threatened, defensive, and inclined to respond with a put-down or accusation of his or her own. Also, these types of accusations ("You did...") do not really provide information about the specific feelings of the unhappy spouse. Neither do the accusations provide any specific suggestions for how to solve the problem.

Using "I" messages, rather than making accusations, can have a very different effect:

"I was embarrassed when ......"

"I felt really stressed out when ...."

Using "I" messages can help your partner better understand and empathize with how you feel. This makes a partner feel less like he or she is being attacked and the conflict discussion becomes more productive.

For example, Lynette and Craig are experiencing substantial conflict over bedtime routines.

"You are so selfish," Lynette charges. "You don't care if I get any sleep or not. You make me so mad when you stay up watching television after I have gone to bed. You know with the television being on the other side of our bedroom wall, I can hear everything. And you don't even bother to turn it down."

Lynette's approach made Craig angry. He insisted that he had been turning the volume down and asked her why she always had to go to bed so early anyway.

The interaction could have been very different if Lynette had used an "I" message and said something like:

"I have really been feeling tired and worn out lately because I can't get to sleep. The sound of the television keeps me awake. It would really help me if you would turn the television down much lower and perhaps move your chair closer to the television so you don't need it as loud for you to hear."

Identify the Best Solution

Couples with happy, lasting marriages are good at identifying the different options available to them for solving their conflicts. Sometimes it is helpful to write all the options down on paper and discuss each one. It can be a source of encouragement and hope just to realize there are different solutions and courses of action available. This reinforces the couple's confidence that they "can work it out." They put their energies into identifying and evaluating alternative solutions instead of attacking each other. Distressed couples are much more limited and narrow in their view of the available options. They are less skilled at thinking of solutions in part because they are more occupied with attacking each other and defending themselves.

CHOOSE THE RIGHT TIME

Conflicts are more likely to be resolved successfully if adequate time is taken to discuss the problem. Conflicts linger and may become more negative when spouses do not take the time to talk about all the issues involved. It is also very important to choose the right time to tackle problems.

Sidney and Louise are in disagreement about where to spend their vacation. They begin to discuss this in the morning but must leave for work before they get very far. They resume their discussions late at night. Because they are both tired, they are irritable and end up in a heated argument.

Couples can more successfully resolve conflict when they set aside discussion times that are unhurried and free of distractions. It is also very helpful to choose a time when neither partner is fatigued, hungry, or not feeling well. A couple may also need to end their discussion if either of them is becoming highly emotional and the argument is intensifying. Under these circumstances it is helpful to leave the discussion and return to it later when both partners can be more calm and objective.

BE PATIENT AND COMMITTED

Resolving conflict and problem solving are skills to be learned. As you learn, you and your partner will get better. It takes time. Couples with happy, lasting marriages are patient with each other and with themselves. Distressed couples tend to be very impatient with each other, which only serves to generate more frustration and anger.

Successful couples also keep the vision of their commitment to each other above the specific conflict situations. They have a commitment to each other, the marriage, and also a commitment to resolve their conflict in a way that is beneficial to both. They are willing to make sacrifices for each other and to do things (sometimes that they don't wish to do) because these are important to the needs of a spouse. Happy couples maintain the perspective that they are both on the same side and that there is never a winner in a conflict. Both either win more intimacy or both lose it. Their ability to focus on the larger and more important vision of their regard for and commitment to each other helps to keep conflict in perspective and makes conflict resolution more successful.

Chapter 4

KEEPING ROMANCE IN YOUR MARRIAGE

O ne of the most striking characteristics of couples with happy, lasting marriages is that they have kept romance in their relationship through the years. Not only is the "spark" still there among these couples, it seems to have grown deeper and brighter over the years.

In contrast, many other couples start their marriages with a strong degree of romantic intimacy, but they seem gradually to lose it, sometimes even becoming very distant from each other as time passes. "All the romance is gone from our marriage," they might say. They are wrong. The romance is not really gone. It has been submerged. It just needs to be cultivated and brought to the surface.

What is the difference between couples who keep romance and those who do not? In order to answer this question we must first ask, "What is romance?"

OPENING OURSELVES TO ROMANCE

Artist and author, Thomas Kinkade, defines romance in a way that describes how romance is manifested in the relationships of the successful couples in our Marriage Success Research Project. Romance, Kinkade states, is not hearts, flowers and violins, although these things can certainly be an enjoyable part of a romantic interlude. Romance is rather a way of encountering the world, a set of habits, an attitude. We are romantic, Kinkade shares, when savoring an experience is a priority for us and when we are willing to invest time and energy into making our experiences more memorable and vivid.[1]

Romance is inside each one of us and is expressed when we open ourselves to experiences and activities that we really enjoy. For example, Nick enjoys sitting in his backyard in the late afternoon and watching the birds come in to the birdfeeders. He delights in their variety of flight, movement, and color.

It is a simple activity, but it provides an opportunity for a special experience. There is beauty in the world around us. Romance comes into your life when you open yourself to savor those special moments.

As we open ourselves to romance in our individual lives we are more capable of sharing romance with our spouses. Our romantic moments are influenced by what we enjoy, what makes us feel alive, and what makes us feel safe and loved. These are unique for each of us as individuals. Couples who enjoy a high degree of romance are very adept at learning and becoming responsive to these unique characteristics and inclinations in each other.

INCREASING ROMANCE

We can increase the romance in our marriages. There are a number of specific ways the happy couples in our Marriage Success Research Project keep romance in their relationships.

MAKING THE ORDINARY INTO
THE EXTRAORDINARY

Sometimes the smallest happenings can bring the greatest enjoyment and satisfaction. Romantic events do not have to be as grand and dashing as a trip to Vienna to be meaningful. Our happily married couples consistently talked about the ordinary, simple activities which add romance to their lives.

"He kisses me every morning before we leave for work," shares a Pennsylvania wife. "He often will call me at lunch and ask me how my day has been."

A Louisiana husband explained, "My wife does a lot of simple things that let me know she cares. For example, I have lower back problems and she regularly massages my back. Last year she sent my parents a card on my birthday, congratulating them on raising a great guy."

"He periodically leaves love notes for me on the refrigerator," shares an Idaho wife. "That makes me feel very special."

"He listens to me," said a Montana wife. "He acts like listening to me is the most important thing in his life and he has all the time in the world for that purpose. I really appreciate that and to me it is very romantic."

"My wife knows how much I enjoy playing tennis," states a Missouri husband. "She took tennis lessons so we could play together."

"She loves to cook and she knows how much I enjoy her cooking," said an Arizona husband. "So she puts a lot of energy and time into preparing these wonderful meals."

"We have been married for 20 years," related a Wisconsin wife. "During that time, I don't think he has ever failed to say, 'Thank you for cooking that fine meal.'"

The marriages of these happy couples are testimony to the fact that romance can be shared in simple, ordinary events. These couples take the ordinary in their daily routines and create extraordinary, meaningful experiences.

BEING SPONTANEOUS

Doing the unplanned and being completely spontaneous can be fun. More spontaneous interaction between husbands and wives can bring great satisfaction in marriage. The word "spontaneous" is derived from a Latin word that means "coming from within." Spontaneous interaction involves a sharing of inner feelings, thoughts, and ideas in which the inner self of one person reaches out to the inner self of another. This type of interaction is free of calculation, routine, and formality. Just a small increase in spontaneity in marriage can do much to create a more positive atmosphere in the relationship.

One factor that prevents couples from being more spontaneous is that they become victims of habit in their interaction and daily routines. They move through each day, day after day, doing the same things. Another factor that minimizes spontaneity is the tendency to postpone joy experiences in the present until our work is done or for possible gain in the future. In too many instances joy experiences are postponed for no real reason except that we have fallen into the habit of "putting off" enjoyment.

Many couples are addicted to the "putting off" habit. They postpone joy experiences for years, retire, and then find they cannot enjoy their retirement. They have postponed so often that they have forgotten how to relax and have fun.

If we allow ourselves to become more spontaneous we will be less likely to "put off" joy experiences and more likely to bring romance into our marriage relationships. The happy couples in our Marriage Success Research Project shared many examples of how spontaneous behavior brought more romance into their marriages.

"Whenever we attend a wedding, Andy proposes to me and I accept," said Inez. "Then when we are going home from the wedding we repeat our wedding vows to each other."

"Sometimes when I come in from work, Dan will hand me a note in an envelope which says, 'I am taking you out to dinner and a movie tonight,' " shared Denise. "It is always a treat and I always love it!"

"On Friday afternoon I sometimes get quite an unexpected

adventure from my wife," said Jay. "She will say to me, 'Don't ask any questions. Just get in the car.' She drives and never tells me where we are going until we get there. Once it was a bed and breakfast place in the mountains. The fishing was great; I love to fish and hike in the woods. It was a fantastic weekend."

"I love mysteries," said Mark. "So when Alexis reads in the paper that there is a mystery play at our local theater, she surprises me with tickets to the play. On one occasion she had me look for clues around the house to find my surprise gift. Each clue I found gave me some hints to find the next clue until I finally found the tickets."

"Some of our most fun times are when we do something on the spur of the moment," said Cliff. "It may seem totally crazy to anyone else, but it will be fun to us. One example is the time we decided to fill a tub with water and bob for apples. Afterwards we made caramel apples together."

Gary describes the spontaneous behavior of his wife which brings him a great deal of joy. "Debbie declares one day a month as Gary's Special Day. She may cook my favorite dish. We will do something special that I particularly enjoy. Basically, she just fills that day with my favorite activities, foods and music."

"Some nights we will go out in the backyard, put our folding chairs back as far as they will go, just lie down side by side and talk as we look up at the stars," shares an Alabama wife. "Some nights we keep count of the shooting stars. This is always unplanned. We never know we're going to do this until we do it."

SHOWING APPRECIATION

Nothing is more important in generating and sustaining romance than the expression of appreciation. William James, a famous psychologist and philosopher, once wrote a book on human needs. Some years after the book was published, he commented that he had forgotten to include one of the most important needs of all – the need for appreciation.

The records of marriage and family counseling clinics suggest that many – perhaps most – marital complaints and problems stem from a lack of feeling appreciated. As one wife stated, "If my husband would just see my good points. . . if he would recognize the worthy things I do and compliment me or let me know he is aware of what I do, it would make me feel much better about myself. As it is, he just complains and criticizes."

How do you think her husband's lack of appreciation and criticism make her feel toward him and the marriage relationship? Does it make her feel romantic? The husband's behavior is self-defeating if he wants romance.

Many of the most intense conflicts and quarrels in marriage grow out of one or both partners feeling unappreciated. Consider the following example.

Husband: I came home from work and told my wife the good news about the congratulations I had just received from my boss for the big project I had finished. She said she was real happy, but she sounded very disinterested. She immediately started chatting about something else. This hurt me and made me sort of mad. I suggested that we go to a movie that night to celebrate. Just as we were leaving, she started listing all the things I needed to fix and do around the house. I became angry and told her to forget about the movie. I was so mad I had to leave the house for a while.

Counselor: Why do you suppose that made you so angry? Of course, you were already a little angry before that happened.

Husband: I think...well, I know that I expected her to show some appreciation for my accomplishment. When she didn't even appear interested, this hurt me. Then when she started telling about all the things I hadn't done, and needed to do, I just exploded.

The happy couples in our Marriage Success Research Project have developed the art of expressing appreciation to each other. They have developed the habit of looking for each other's strengths and then communicating their simple pleasure in, and gratitude for, those strengths. By doing this they enhance each other's self-esteem. They naturally are more likely then to feel good about themselves, each other, and the relationship. And in this way, romance is enhanced.

"Bob sends me roses once a month," said Edna. "He has been doing this for the last 25 years. It makes me feel very desirable. I think he is the most romantic man that I know. But more important to me than the roses is when he calls me and says, 'I love you.' He sometimes tells me he loves me in sign language."

"It is not unusual for Ron to cook our meals," said Colleen. "But sometimes he will make those meals so romantic. Last week he had candlelight and soft music and left a card by my place. When I opened the card, it read, 'I am lucky to be married to such a wonderful woman!' Yeah, I like that."

Kent, a Californian, shares a quality of his wife which has had positive consequences for his self-esteem and his romantic feelings toward her. "I've got plenty of faults," said Kent, "but Carla just gives her attention to my good qualities. She sees them better than I do. She gives me sincere compliments in private and in front of other people. It gives me a lot of confidence. And I tell you, I love her for it. It's a joy to live with this woman."

It was their fifth wedding anniversary. Rob opened his card from Michelle. It read: "How do I love you? Let me count the ways. I love you because you have an enthusiasm for life. I love you because you are patient and kind. I love you because you are fun to be with. I love you because you are unselfish. I love you because you bring out the best in me. . . But most of all I love you because you are you."

Rob regards this card as one of the nicest gifts he has ever received. This anniversary card meant a great deal to Rob because the words of appreciation in it affirmed him. They built him up psycho-logically. They let him know that Michelle loves him, that she sees his many good traits and that she appreciates them.

Expressing sincere appreciation communicates the message, "You are a person of worth and dignity. You have much to contribute to others." Expressing appreciation also communicates the message, "I am interested in you; I see and acknowledge your positive qualities."

At the heart of appreciation is the ability to pay attention to another person, and that is why it is so vital to enhancing romance in the marriage relationship. The reason that many people do not express appreciation is because they are extremely self-centered or preoccupied with themselves. Couples who have happy, lasting marriages pay a lot of attention to each other. Their expressions of appreciation to each other bring a harvest of romance to their relationship.

PLANNING FOR GOOD TIMES

Les and Jean had been married for four years when they came for counseling about the possibility of getting divorced. After the first few sessions the counselor said, "I don't see a major problem in your marriage. I mean you both love each other. You don't have any serious conflict. Your relationship seems to be going smoothly on a day-to-day basis. What do you think is the problem?"

Jean paused for a moment before answering, "When you look at it logically I guess there is not any major problem. Except that the spark is gone. We just seem to have lost interest in each other."

"The passion is not there," added Les.

"But the passion was there once?" asked the counselor.

"Yes, it was strong," replied Les.

"We used to have a lot of romantic times when we were dating and early in the marriage," said Jean.

"We did more fun things together," said Les.

"What do you do for fun now?" asked the counselor.

There was a long pause of silence. "Nothing, I guess," answered Jean.

"We do go out and eat sometimes," suggested Les. "I guess that's about it."

"Is there anything you both enjoy that you could do together?" asked the counselor.

After some minutes of pondering the question, Les and Jean agreed that playing board games and hiking were two activities they both enjoyed. The counselor asked the couple to go home and further discuss this issue to see if they could identify other activities they both enjoyed. They were asked to list these mutual interests and prioritize them according to degree of interest or enjoyment. After completing this exercise they were given the assignment of doing two of these activities together each week. They were encouraged to plan the activities ahead so that they were scheduled and would be more similar to dates. After six months of participating in this experiment, Jean and Les found the enjoyment of their relationship had returned. They felt close to each other again; romance and interest were renewed.

Many couples drift apart because they stop spending time together and because they allow themselves to get into routines where they rarely do anything fun or pleasant together. Happy couples with lasting marriages spend a lot of time doing fun, pleasurable activities together. They plan many of these activities, and they look forward to them as dates. So there is anticipation of these times together just as there was when they were courting each other before marriage.

Couples with happy marriages plan these pleasant times together in a variety of forms. Some are expensive. Others cost nothing.

"We really enjoy going to the movies. Usually we eat out at a restaurant before or after the movie. But we always plan to start early enough that we are not rushed. That helps us to have a relaxed evening that we can savor."

"Getting away on an overnight trip somewhere three or four times during the year helps us to feel closer and renews the flame. It is so much easier to give each other our full attention when we are away from our daily routine and don't have to answer the telephone, pay bills, and do household chores."

"I think our most enjoyable times together are the activities that don't cost anything. We like to pack a picnic and go to the local park or to a favorite spot of ours by the river. We love to spend a cozy evening playing cards and drinking hot chocolate."

But isn't it difficult to have "dates" when a couple has children and all the demands of home and work? According to the happy couples in our Marriage Success Research Project, it is not as great a challenge as is commonly assumed. These couples meet the challenge by planning their "dates" just as they schedule everything else.

"We set aside every Friday night as our date night," said Penny. "We enjoy basketball so we get season tickets. We also get season tickets to the local theatre. Getting the season tickets motivates us to carry through with our dates. With that much money invested we aren't going to allow something else to take priority over our date.

"We don't need that motivation as much now," she explained. "But a few years ago with three children and everything else that was going on in our lives we did need it because there were always 'reasons' to postpone the dates. I think it is one of the best investments we make."

Many of our couples mentioned that they enjoyed watching sunsets together or taking walks together. Some enjoy morning coffee and conversation or lunch for two. Pleasant, fun activities do not need to be elaborate or expensive.

EXPRESSING KINDNESS AND CONSIDERATION

The happily married couples in our Marriage Success Research Project consistently reported that acts of kindness and consideration play a very important role in creating an atmosphere of romance in the marriage relationship. Kindness and consideration reflect the presence of a high regard for each other and respect for the differences in each other. Both are essential for romance and marriage happiness.

The ability to respect differences in each other enhances romance and positive feelings about the relationship. Respecting differences also prevents much conflict and resentment. Many people regard habits, interests, ways of thinking, and views of others that differ greatly from their own as inferior or wrong. This inclination causes resentment, frustration, conflict, and deterioration in romance.

Shawn grew up in a family that always had numerous projects going on. His mother was an artist and continually had paintings in progress. His dad enjoyed knifemaking as a hobby and usually had materials spread out in the family room as well as in the garage.

Shawn was an avid rock hound and often had his rock collections out.

Shawn's wife, Dana, was reared in a home where any projects such as woodworking, crafts, or painting were done in a workshop in the garage. The family rule was that all work and play areas must be cleaned up every time they were used.

Now Shawn and Dana's different views about keeping house are causing conflict. Dana complains that Shawn is slovenly. Shawn resents her nagging at him to clean up and tells her that she is compulsively neat.

Both Shawn and Dana feel criticized and inferior. They have slipped into a pattern of negative interaction by criticizing and judging each other because of differences with regard to house-keeping patterns.

The challenge for this couple is to respect their differences and to realize that they are, after all, simply differences. The differences do not indicate inferiority or character flaws. Shawn is not less worthy because his attitude about clutter is casual. Dana is not compulsive because she likes order. They are simply different. She can demonstrate kindness to him by overlooking his projects in progress; he can be considerate and tidy up a bit more often.

Kindness expresses itself in many different forms among happy couples. It is remembering anniversaries, birthdays, and other special occasions. It is a hug when one of you is feeling sad. It is speaking words of encouragement. It is stopping to listen when your partner really needs to talk.

"I have a very stressful job," said Denny. "Talking with Dawn about the problems at work is the best stress reliever I have. It also helps me get a clearer perspective on those issues and make better decisions. With a house and kids, Dawn always has a never-ending list of tasks to complete. But she always drops what she is doing and listens. She gives me her total attention. She will ask good questions that sometimes help me to see something in a new light. She is not only my wife. She is my best friend."

"Reading is something I have always done with enthusiasm. I recently developed vision problems because of mucular degeneration," said Daryl. "Mary reads to me every day – sometimes until her voice gives out."

"I was very close to my mother," said Barbara. "She passed on about a year ago following a long illness. It has been real hard for me. My husband started a scholarship in memory of my mother at the community college where she taught. It means so much to me and has helped me get through this difficult time. She would be very proud."

Pamela is a manager whose work periodically becomes hectic. She talks about how the kindness and consideration of her husband during one of those times was a lifesaver for her. "He pitched in and helped me with a lot of the paperwork that had to be done. He worked with me every evening for over a week. He also cooked dinner every evening during that time."

Jan is 32 years old and is undergoing cancer treatment which has caused her to lose her hair. "One of the biggest surprises I have ever had was the night that Lance came in with his head shaved," said Jan. "I had no idea he was going to do that. It made me feel very close to him."

"I had been having a really tough time at work," shared Peggy. "Some very negative things were going on and I had no control over them. I was discouraged and frustrated.

"One evening, I came in after a particularly bad day and just sat down and cried," she said. "Later that evening my husband, Bob, came in and surprised me with a gift. He had bought a suit for me that I had spotted during one of our recent strolls through the mall. I really liked it but had not bought it at the time because I thought we needed to spend the money on other things.

"When Bob gave that suit to me it lifted my spirits more than words can express. It was so sweet of him. I always feel beautiful when I wear that suit. It is a special memory, and one of the most romantic moments I have known."

These examples are but a few of the acts of kindness and consideration that fill the marriage relationships of these couples. The many expressions of kindness among these couples create an interpersonal atmosphere that leaves each partner feeling loved, important, and supported. Kindness overshadows shortcomings and irritations. It creates an atmosphere where romance can blossom.

Chapter 5

OVERCOMING CHRONIC STRESS AND HASSLES

An old adage says, "It's not the big storms that destroy the great oak tree. It's the little bugs." This is also true in our personal lives. Over the long haul, we experience a much greater degree of harmful stress from the small daily hassles than we do from the major crises or storms in our lives.

Our chronic hassles may include continually spending an excessive amount of time at work, always being in a rush, being trapped in congested traffic everyday, or problems in arranging good childcare. In short, any of the daily things that can – and do – go wrong can become stressors.

THE PILE UP OF CHRONIC STRESS

Most of our daily hassles and frustrations, taken individually, are usually very minor. However, when these "minor" hassles are chronic and they all combine and "pile up" on us, the effect can be severe and very stressful.

Kimball comes home from work every Friday night exhausted. For him and his wife, Juanita, one chronic stressor is the great amount of time and energy he puts into his job. This is particularly frustrating to Kimball because he believes the amount of time and energy demanded by his superiors is excessive. Both Kimball and Juanita are convinced that his job demands are hurting their family life.

Kimball wants to spend more time with Juanita. They had planned a date for this particular Friday night. Kimball had such a busy, hectic day at work that he did not have time to eat lunch. The trip home from work took over two hours because freeway traffic was bumper to bumper. He was stressed out by the time he arrived home.

Juanita's day hadn't been much better. She taught at the university but left a desk stacked with work from the last three or four days – odds and ends needing to be finished. Their four-year-old was crying when Juanita picked her up from the daycare center. Juanita had not been pleased with this particular daycare center for some time but had not yet found a suitable alternative. She felt frustrated and guilty about this situation. Since this was to be a date night with Kimball they had arranged for a babysitter, but Juanita had reservations about leaving their daughter again. After all, she had been in daycare all day and did not want to be left again.

But Juanita knew that Kimball was looking forward to their night out together. She and Kimball needed the time together. Reluctantly, she decided to go forward with the plans for their date.

Juanita and Kimball scurried to get ready to go out. They were running behind because Kimball was late arriving home because of the congested traffic.

As they were about to walk out the door Juanita received a telephone call from one of her students who was having an emergency school problem and was pleading with Juanita for help. Juanita wanted to help; she listened; she asked questions and offered suggestions.

The conversation took time. When Juanita finished and looked at Kimball, she did not like what she saw. He was livid. Angrily, he threw the car keys across the room, and shouted, "Forget the whole thing. There's no point in going now."

Before she could respond, he continued shouting, "You didn't want to go anyway, did you? Why didn't you just tell me you didn't want to go? You don't care anything about being with me!"

Juanita screamed back, "Don't you yell at me! I can't control the fact that this student called me and needed help. Don't blame me. It's not my fault that you were late. You don't sound much like you want to be with me tonight."

This couple is in conflict, shouting at each other and having an unpleasant evening, not because anything is inherently wrong in their relationship but because they are stressed out. On this evening, Juanita and Kimball have become victims, as most of us do, to a pile-up of everyday hassles and stresses.

Chronic stress alters our basic balance or equilibrium by putting demands on us that can leave us emotionally and physically exhausted. We eventually begin to feel that we just can't deal with it anymore. We become increasingly irritable, depressed, negative and tired.

When something stresses us, it places a demand on our psychological and physical resources to deal with it. Our bodies go into a "fight or flight" stage of readiness to meet the challenge. The body pumps adrenaline; blood pressure rises; the heart beat increases; and muscles tense. If we continue in this state over a long period of time because of chronic stress, we eventually reach a point of physical and emotional exhaustion. We become more susceptible to stress-related diseases such as high blood pressure, heart disease, and ulcers.

In a similar way chronic stress can exhaust a marriage relationship of its resources, causing the interaction and feeling to become more negative. As chronic stress upsets the balance or equilibrium of the relationship, it causes a sickness and slow dying in the marriage that neither partner completely understands.

THE STRESSFUL ENVIRONMENT

"One thing that helped us to get our stress under control was when we realized how much of our stress was coming from our environment," said Irene. "It was coming from expectations and values of others around us, the systems and lifestyles we were connected with. When we came to understand what was really causing our stress we were much better able to manage it."

If you think life is more stressful than it used to be, it is not just your runaway imagination. Our society has become much more stressful than was true 40 years ago. There are some fundamental reasons for this increased stress and it is important to the well-being of our marriages to understand those reasons. By knowing the sources of chronic stress in our environment we will be more successful in protecting our marriages from its harmful effects.

MORE WORK AND LESS FREE TIME

This one change alone has contributed much to our stressful lifestyles. Because we are working longer hours we have less leisure time and less time for marriage and family life. It is surprising to see the degree of change that has taken place. For example, in 1935, the free time or "disposable time" for male workers was 40 hours a week. In 1973, it had declined to 26 hours a week and in 1990, it had been reduced to 17 hours a week – less than half what it was in 1935. The amount of free time for women is substantially less than it is for men.[1]

One reason we are working longer and enjoying less free time is that the cost of living continues to rise. Real, spendable income, after taxes and inflation, has not increased in the last 25 years. As a result, many work overtime every chance they get or work a second job just to keep afloat. Many people are also working long and hard to pay off mortgages, large credit card debts, and car loans. Also, more companies are downsizing and adopting the philosophy of doing more (work) with less (workers). They are inclined to increase the burdens of employees, asking one person to do the work of two or three.

MATERIALISM

Our culture places high value on materialism. According to the way our society rewards people with status and esteem, the most important criteria for judging a person's worth are a person's success in a career or job and how much money he or she makes.

As a consequence, a growing number of people place their highest priority on career and job success. What drives that priority is often a desire to accumulate things. Advertisers and the media constantly bombard us with the message that to be worthy we should accumulate things. Carefully crafted commercials tell us that if we buy this product we will be more sexually attractive. If we buy that product we will have class and status. Skillfully they convince us that by purchasing a more expensive product we somehow become more successful and happy.

So whether it's a bigger house, a new car, or expensive clothes, we want more and more and never feel satisfied. We work hard at our careers and jobs so that we can buy these things. Then we work very hard under considerable stress to pay our ballooning debts.

Being caught in materialism adds a great amount of stress to daily life. It takes a toll on a marriage relationship and other relationships as well. We feel pressured, discontent, and discouraged because the nature of materialism is that we never feel that we have enough.

One of the greatest threats to our marriage relationships is that we get so involved in this materialistic quest that we don't have time for the most important things in our lives – relationships. We sadly neglect our marriage relationships and the relationships with our children.

THE HURRIED PACE

"We are on a dead run from the time we get up in the morning until we go to bed at night," said a Kansas wife. "Everything we do is in a hurry. I get pretty sick of it."

Technological advances have brought us many wonderful benefits and conveniences. However, they have also contributed greatly to the hurried pace of life – which adds to our stress. The computer, the FAX machine, e-mail, and voice mail all offer promises of making our work easier and less time consuming. But they actually have led to the expectations that we will be able to do our work so much faster that we will do a much greater volume of work. People expect responses or information by e-mail and FAX on their desks in a matter of minutes – not days.

We watch television programs and routinely see problems solved in 30 minutes or an hour. We are so accustomed to going to fast food places and having a meal served to us in four minutes or less that we become impatient with the idea of preparing a meal from scratch.

All of this adds to our levels of stress and spills over into our marriages. We try to hurry our marriage relationships like we do everything else. We expect that marriage satisfaction should be instant (and problems instantly gone) and when they are not, we become dissatisfied and impatient. We set ourselves up for failure and find that we grow more and more dissatisfied and disillusioned because the intimacy we seek cannot be hurried or rushed. Intimacy takes time.

LESS SECURITY AND STABILITY

During the last 40 years the total environment has become less secure and stable. For one thing, family instability has increased. Divorce affects many families; large numbers of children are spending their childhoods in single-parent homes.

Job security has, to a large extent, become just a memory from the past. Downsizing has become a common corporate practice. As companies increasingly restructure or relocate, security and stability are shaken.

"The company I have been with for 12 years is relocating to Mexico," said a Colorado husband. "They want me to stay with them and have even offered an incentive to stay. But, of course I would have to move to Mexico. We don't want to leave our friends and relatives.

Our roots are here. But even if I don't relocate to Mexico I will probably still have to move my family to a different community in the United States. It is certainly causing us a lot of worry."

A Michigan husband being transferred to the west coast and his wife face the difficult dilemma of what to do about her career. "Her income is higher than mine and her position is more stable," he shares. "We don't know what is the best way to handle this, but we really need both jobs. We have decided that for now I will move to the west coast and she will stay here. We plan to make a lot of telephone calls and one of us will fly to see the other once a month. It's not going to be easy. There doesn't seem to be any good answer to this situation."

THE ALL-YOU-CAN-EAT-BUFFET MENTALITY

Each of us experiences a great amount of emotional and physical stress on a regular basis just from the volume of things to do each day. "The list of things to get done is unending," observed a Virginia wife. "Our list includes taking our kids to daycare early in the morning, going to work, picking the kids up from childcare after we get off work, running errands, housework, cooking, paying bills, gardening, going to exercise class, pet care, being involved in our church, playing tennis twice a week, and being involved in some community activities. This is not everything we do – just examples I can think of right now."

Your list of daily activities may look very different from hers. However, you would probably be shocked at the length of it.

Imagine an all-you-can-eat buffet offering many delicious foods. You may experience stress from this wonderful experience in three different ways. First, there are many attractive options from which to choose. You have the dilemma of choosing between foods you really want and those dishes you like less but you know are healthier. Second, you may try to avoid the stress of choosing by eating everything; you will certainly experience the strain of overeating. Third, even if you make wise selections you may experience some stress due to feelings of deprivation over foods that you didn't choose (or have room for).

In a similar way we are faced with many options from which to choose concerning how we spend our time. There are many activities we must do, while many others are optional. The many options for how we spend our time have mushroomed during the last 50 years just as the choices concerning the features you desire in your toothpaste and automobile tires have multiplied. The sheer volume of choices contributes to complex decision-making and adds to our stress level.

As in the all-you-can-eat buffet, we often try to do it all in our daily lives. We take on more than we realistically can do, thus keeping ourselves in a chronic state of pressure and demands. An Ohio wife shares, "I have been frustrated because I have not been able to make much progress on a number of projects I want to complete. I was determined I would get them done, so I made a detailed schedule of when I would do what. I reserved between 6:30 p.m. and 8:00 p.m. for one activity. I would work on another project from 8:00 p.m. to 9:30 p.m. and so on. What just shocked me and completely changed my perspective," she continued, "was that when I put all this down on paper I realized for the first time that it was literally impossible for me to get all these things done. There aren't enough hours in a day. I was trying to do what could not be done and feeling bad about it."

Why do we do this to ourselves? Perhaps because we think we should or we try to keep up with someone else. Many of us take on too much because we have an interest in many things and we have a hearty appetite for life. Many of us have bought into the belief that the more we do the more worthy we are.

Whatever the reasons, we are presented with opportunities to become involved in a multitude of time-consuming activities. We easily become overloaded. Our stress level goes up. We feel inadequate, frustrated, irritable, even angry because we cannot do it all. Too often these negative feelings are turned on a spouse and marriage satisfaction declines.

SUCCESSFULLY MANAGING CHRONIC STRESS

We don't have to be victims of the unending hassles and pressures of daily life. Effective strategies for managing chronic stress can prevent it from harming your health or your marriage. Happy couples with lasting marriages have shared some successful ways of managing chronic stress.

GET OUT OF THE STRESSFUL ENVIRONMENT

Often our chronic stress is primarily due to the circumstances we're in. We may have little or no control over the conditions in the environment. Sometimes the only way to reduce such stress substantially is to remove ourselves from the stressful environment. Our successful couples did not hesitate to take this step to protect their individual health and the health of their marriages.

Rod and Annie had lived in Arkansas all their lives. A big promotion came to Rod which necessitated their moving to Los Angeles. They were excited about the career advancement, the substantial increase in salary, and a new part of the country in which to live.

The stressful nature of their new environment quickly took its toll. Rod and Annie missed their old network of friends and family back home. They felt isolated. They had experienced a strong sense of belonging and connection in their Arkansas community. Now, they felt absolutely no sense of community in their new environment.

"The financial stress was unbelievable," recalled Rod. "We knew the cost of living would be higher in Los Angeles, but we were not prepared for how much higher. Insurance premiums doubled and mortgage payments tripled for a house comparable to what we had in Arkansas. The property taxes were four times higher. If there is such a thing as economic terror we began to have it. We had to borrow sizeable amounts of money just to pay our bills and we certainly were not living extravagantly."

Rod and Annie suffered substantial physical and emotional stress as a result of their two-hour commute to and from work every day. The nature of the commute – the slow, stop-and-go, bumper-to-bumper crawl each day – was as distressing as the large amount of time on the road.

"We worried about the crime rate," said Annie. "It was so much higher than what we had ever known. We were concerned about this environment for raising our children."

"One Saturday afternoon we were taking a walk and talking about all these things and we came to an important decision," said Rod. "We had lived in the Los Angeles area for two years and we had not enjoyed it. Our quality of life had declined. We were spending less time together as a couple and as a family. Our day-to-day living conditions were hurting our family.

"We concluded that life was too short to continue to live this way and that our marriage and family were far more important than my career. We made the decision to leave and return to Arkansas. We have never regretted that decision."

WEAR ONE HAT AT A TIME

Because our list of daily duties is long, we often try to do three or four things all at once. This is stressful and frustrating. Darlene, for example, is wearing three hats at 8:00 at night. First, she is wearing her parent hat, listening to her daughter talk about her day at school and ask for help with her math homework. But Darlene isn't doing a good job of wearing the parent hat because she is only half listening to her daughter. She is also wearing her career hat and is preoccupied with a report she must prepare for presentation at work. In her hostess hat, Darlene is preparing a grocery list for their dinner party the next night. No wonder she snaps at her husband when he comes in and begins to talk with her about a trip to the mountains he would like to take.

"One strategy I have found to be particularly helpful in managing stress is to strive to wear only one hat at a time," advised Kathy. "When I'm at home with my husband and children I try to leave my work hat at the office and give my full attention to my family."

While it is not always possible to avoid wearing multiple hats, setting one hat at a time as a goal and making it a general practice can reduce much stress. It allows you to focus your attention and energy and to avoid fragmentation.

REDUCE THE LOAD AND PRIORITIZE

A prominent quality of the couples in our national Marriage Success Research Project is that they are skilled in reducing their load and in prioritizing as to what is really important. Time together as a couple tops the list of what is truly important and they structure their lifestyles in accordance with that priority.

"We learned this the hard way," shared Casey. "The first three years of our marriage were relaxed and with few responsibilities. We spent most of our time with each other and did a lot of fun things.

"Then we had children and, as the years went by, we became more involved in our careers and church. Our load became heavier. It reached a peak when we had been married for ten years."

That was the year that Casey and Lindy knew they had to change something if they wanted their marriage to be as fulfilling as they desired. "That year Lindy was president of our local PTA and vice president of a professional organization," remembered Casey. "I was an officer in the Kiwanis Club and the Lions Club. We both were on the board of directors for another community organization. We belonged to a health club and went there two or three times a week.

"We were actively involved in our church. I was a deacon and both Lindy and I were serving on multiple church committees. She was in a bowling league and had a commitment to bowl once a week. I played golf with friends most Saturdays. We both had taken on extra responsibilities in our jobs.

"I began to have blood pressure problems for the first time in my life," shared Casey. "Lindy had bronchitis that went to pneumonia. We were always exhausted. We never had a quiet moment together."

"We finally realized that we were stressed out because we were doing too much. We had to let some things go," Lindy added. "We talked a long time about what was really important to us. That was spending time together and we weren't doing a good job of that.

"So we reorganized our lifestyle," she continued. "We dropped several things from our list of commitments: bowling, golf, the board of directors, a church committee, for instance. It made a big difference. It gave us back some time and energy and made our lives more relaxed and pleasant. The benefit to our marriage and our personal happiness was enormous."

KEEP RHYTHM

In Ann Lindbergh's book, *Gift From the Sea,*[2] she shares about a very difficult time in her life when she feared she was becoming emotionally disturbed. Her life was stressed out, fast-paced, and busy: She had come to the point of exhaustion.

To protect her health and her sanity, she retreated to the beach for several days. She went there alone and after a few days had passed, she lost much of her tenseness. She became aware of the life around her as she watched the tide come in and go out, walked the beach, and collected shells. Each day had a rhythm such as the tide rolling in and then returning to the sea.

She became deeply aware that life and nature have a rhythm. A flash of insight revealed to her that her major problem was that her life lacked rhythm. For a long time she had been caught up in a nonstop series of hurried behavior, appointments, projects, and deadlines. Fun-filled pauses and relaxing breaks had been nonexistent. Ann Lindbergh eventually restored her rhythm and emotional health by incorporating frequent creative pauses of refreshing and relaxing activities. It is also very important to the health and happiness of a marriage to keep a rhythm and to incorporate creative pauses of refreshing, recreational, and relaxing activities. Creative pauses that keep rhythm in our lives might be taking a trip, taking a walk around the neighborhood, playing cards or board games, watching fireflies on a summer evening, hiking in the woods, or playing golf. They can be anything that refreshes, restores, and relaxes us.

"Barry and I were drifting apart," confessed Rhonda. "Part of it was because we weren't together enough. We were too busy with other parts of our lives. Another reason was because we didn't have anything left for each other when we were together.

"We were exhausted," she continued. "We were tense and irritable. I did not know what was in Barry's mind and heart and he did not know what was in mine because we were always in a hurry.

"It's not surprising that we were not very happy," Rhonda said. "But we had enough sense to realize, after hours of talking about it, that we were not unhappy with each other but we were unhappy with the way we were living. And we knew we could change the way we were living."

The relationship between Rhonda and Barry regained its vitality and happiness. A number of creative pauses they incorporated gave their marriage some rhythm. Two daily creative pauses seem to have had a surprisingly beneficial influence on their personal well-being and the health of their marriage.

"We both love jigsaw puzzles. We keep a card table set up with one of those big, challenging puzzles in progress. We find little bits of time – 15 or 20 minutes – to work on it," Rhonda explained.

"Most days we also work in our yard together. We pull weeds or plant flowers and talk. It is good exercise, too."

Frequent creative pauses are important because they add rhythm to life and marriage. They allow us to rediscover the joy, mystery, and wonder of our lives together. The couples with happy, lasting marriages are very good at maintaining rhythm in their day-to-day experiences.

SIMPLIFY LIFE

The complexities of modern life create much stress for us. Whenever we simplify our lives we can substantially reduce our stress. The couples who participated in our Marriage Success Research Project were skilled at simplifying their lives.

Len and Gail owned a beautiful home in the country. They had a 20-mile commute each way to town where they worked. "The drive every day really got old," said Len. "A large area of our land had to be mowed: So I was continually mowing. The house and the acreage required a lot of time to maintain. It was a constant struggle for us.

"It was a beautiful place but I guess living out in the country was not quite as enjoyable to us as it is to many people," he continued. "Anyway, we sold the acreage and moved to town. Our new house is much smaller and easier to keep up. The yard requires very little work. We live close enough that we can both ride our bicycles to work. It has really simplified our lives."

Many couples shared that they simplified their lives and reduced stress by limiting what they tried to do each day and by focusing on a few specific goals. "I find that one of the best strategies for keeping my stress level down is to have no more than four goals for each day," advised Lela.

"I say to myself in the early morning, 'These are the four goals I have for this day.' It helps to organize my day and it's manageable," said Lela. "I don't try to do a lot of other things. And I have a feeling of satisfaction at accomplishing those four goals. I feel better about myself.

"I used to try to do too many things each day," shared Lela. "And I had a chronic feeling of failure because there was no way I could get it all done."

There are many ways we may simplify our lives that most of us never even think about. One example that many couples reported is mealtime.

Anita and Reggie share an example of how they simplified their lives in this particular area. "Eating out is more stressful for us than preparing meals at home," said Anita. "I mean, when we eat out we seem to have trouble deciding where we want to go. Then traffic and parking can be a hassle getting there. It can be irritating if there is a long wait or when the restaurant is crowded. It's expensive to eat out so the financial strain makes us feel bad, too.

"We simplified our lives by making the decision to eat most of our meals at home and by eating out only occasionally," Anita said. "We simplified the meal preparation by cooking most of the meals for the week on a Saturday. We might grill several chickens, fix a large casserole and a big pot of chili, for example. This gives us something to take for our lunches at work and when we come home in the evenings all we have to do is warm up our dinner. This has saved us considerable time, money and aggravation."

NURTURE

Couples who prevent chronic hassles from becoming an overwhelming burden consistently utilize one other important strategy. They give each other the gift of nurture. They take good care of themselves and each other. The gift of nurture includes regular exercise; eating a healthy, nutritious diet; getting enough rest; and cultivating positive thought patterns.

"We work out with weights three days a week and do brisk walking three days of the week," said one husband. "We can literally feel the worries of the day slipping away as we go through our exercise routines.

"Exercise makes us feel stronger and more like we can handle whatever challenges come our way," he said. "Daily frustrations just don't bother us as much when we work out."

Exercise is one of the most powerful neutralizers of stress. It is also one of the safest and best tranquilizers. Exercise is a very effective way to release pent-up frustrations and tensions.

Many couples report using relaxation techniques. Peaceful imagery and meditation in which a person visualizes peaceful scenes contribute significantly to a relaxed state of mind.

A Texas husband shares a visual image he has found to be effective in reducing his stress and tension.

"First I prepare my room with some aroma therapy spray or candles that remind me of the sea. Then I stretch out, close my eyes and breathe deeply," he said. "I visualize myself walking beside the ocean on a lonely beach. I hear the sound of large, powerful waves breaking and seagulls calling above me.

"The ocean is clear blue and periodically a dolphin jumps out of the water. A couple of pelicans lazily dive into the ocean looking for their lunch. Sunshine warms my whole body. The warm sand soothes my feet.

"I can take as much time as I wish walking along this beach. I am not in a hurry. I feel totally relaxed and at peace."

The successful couples in our research also have a positive life philosophy and positive thought patterns. This quality is important in helping them to overcome daily stress and hassles.

How stressful or frustrating an event is depends largely on our perception of it. Those who have an optimistic, hopeful attitude are more likely to manage stress well.

Some of us seem to be naturally inclined to be optimistic and others of us are inclined to be pessimistic. The author of *Conquering Stress*, K.R.S. Edstrom, suggests that some individuals are designed with cat-sleeping-in-the-sun-like reflexes (seldom in a hurry, slow to anger, easy going) while others are equipped with turned-up-rabbit-like tendencies (always in a hurry, easily angered, hard driving and competitive). Some people seem to be better designed by their temperament to deal with stress.

Regardless of how we may be naturally inclined to respond to stress or how we may have learned to deal with stress, each of us can learn to respond more effectively by cultivating positive thought patterns. Thought patterns are reflected in the ways that we talk to ourselves and may be either positive or negative. Our self-talk may add to our stress or reduce it.

Our specific self-talk and thought patterns are driven by the assumptions or beliefs (which are not necessarily correct) we carry around with us. Some common negative beliefs or assumptions which cause negative self-talk include:

- Everyone must like me and approve of me.
- My self-worth depends completely on my achievement. I must be perfect in everything I do.

- People who respect me must agree with me.

We need often to examine our basic assumptions about life. If we discover that we are carrying counter-productive beliefs such as those mentioned above, we can replace them with more realistic and positive beliefs such as:

- It is not necessary that everyone likes me. I am fortunate that some people like me and that I have a few good friends.
- My worth as a person is much more than my specific achievement and does not depend on my accomplishment. I do not have to be perfect in order to be worthy.
- It is not necessary for people to agree with me in order to respect me. We are all different. It is normal and acceptable to disagree.

Those couples who deal successfully with stress have developed the art of positive thinking. They have cultivated a pattern of positive self-talk. They remind themselves of their own strengths and resources rather than dwelling on their limitations. They emphasize the positive aspects of a situation. A positive approach to life is developed which creates self-confidence, optimism, and hope.

Chapter 6

NAVIGATING DANGEROUS WATERS:
How to Manage Finances
How to Love Your In-Laws

In romance novels and fairy tales, the newly married couple sail blissfully over calm waters into the sunset. In real life, things seldom happen so well or so easily.

All married couples are going to encounter difficult times and circumstances – no matter how compatible they are or how much in love. Couples who are successful have learned to chart a course that gets them safely through the dangerous waters of difficulty. Furthermore, they can look back and see how coming through hard times has enriched their marriage. Two very common potential trouble areas are finances and in-laws.

HOW TO MANAGE FINANCES

Take a poll of married couples and ask about the problems they have experienced in marriage. Money would be at the top of the list. Whether it is getting established in a job or buying a house or paying tuition for the children, most couples experience serious financial strain at some point in marriage. Many face major financial challenges throughout marriage.[1]

How can finances be such a problem in these recent years? After all, on a daily basis the news reports have statements that the economy is growing or doing fine. A husband in Oregon expresses the feeling of many, "I am so frustrated by this. If the economy is so good, why are Lynn and I – both of us fortunate to have good jobs – having a hard time making ends meet?"

FINANCIAL STRAIN IN OUR ENVIRONMENT

It just isn't politically correct to talk about the extent of financial strain in America.

The natural preference of politicians and government leaders is to put the best foot forward and emphasize the indicators that show how well our economy is doing. Meanwhile the trends that reflect financial problems are ignored. For example, they will applaud the growth in jobs but won't discuss the low-paying nature of those jobs.

We can avoid some frustration and can better manage our personal finances if we understand the extent and nature of the financial strains in our environment. Consider these points:

- According to Bureau of Census data, over 80 percent of people who retire at age 65 have no savings.
- Real income (that which is spendable after accounting for tax increases and inflation) has not increased in the last 25 years.
- Many consumer items have increased dramatically in cost during the same period that real income has not increased. For example, the median sales price of single family homes

was $23,000 in 1970. In the year 2000 that cost has increased to over $120,000.[2]

SECRETS OF SUCCESSFUL FINANCIAL MANAGEMENT

Much of the financial strain in the environment is beyond our control. We don't have the power to influence interest rates, inflation, or the stock market. This should not discourage us. It does emphasize the importance of managing well our personal finances and the resources which we can control. There are certain principles which successful couples have found to be important in effective financial management.

Direct the Cash Flow

Many couples get into financial trouble because they don't direct where their money is spent with any kind of plan or forethought. They just "let it happen" and the resulting flow of cash sweeps through their lives and directs them. They lose control.

Randall and Janet are a couple who came to the brink of financial disaster in this way. We want to share with you how they turned it around.

"We were powerless over our finances," said Randall. "Our debts were so high that we could not make the monthly payments and still live. Every month we were going about a thousand dollars over our income.

"We thought we would have to file bankruptcy," he continued. "Fortunately, a financial consultant assured us that would not be necessary. He helped us to consolidate our debts to give us much lower monthly payments."

"When the financial consultant asked us exactly how our money was being spent, we couldn't tell him. We had no idea until we pulled together all of our cancelled checks and credit card receipts for the past two months," Randall said. "And we were surprised at what we learned."

"We were writing too many checks and making too many credit card purchases," stated Janet. "We regained mastery of our finances by getting rid of our credit cards and writing no checks. Those were two major changes for us."

"Instead we paid cash for nearly everything. For the first time we always knew how much money we had left in our account. I think this was the most important step that gave us control over our money. Before we would always have checks floating around and we never knew how many were still out." Randall continued, "And with checks and credit cards, it's very easy to spend a lot of money without seeming like you have. Now I can look in my wallet and see exactly how much cash I have to last until payday."

The widespread availability of credit cards and the many buy-now-pay-later opportunities encourage a philosophy of buying everything we want. Unfortunately, this can lead to financial disaster. As Randall observed earlier, it is very easy to spend a lot of money without realizing it with credit purchases.

Couples who are successful at managing their finances are able to acknowledge that they cannot buy everything they would like and so they decide what they need or want most. It is essential to establish priorities in order to manage the flow of money accordingly.

Another practice which can help us to direct cash flow is to put some money each pay period into a temporary savings for emergencies. Unexpected expenses arise for everyone and those who suffer the least are those who are best prepared.

"One of the smartest things we have done over the years is to maintain a savings," said an Iowa husband. "We just had a $900 repair job on our car. Fortunately, we could pay for it out of our savings. If we had not had the savings we would have had to borrow the money. I'm thankful we did not have to do that because we don't need another monthly payment chipping away at our resources."

Savings are a good way to keep financial difficulties to a minimum. Many couples find it helpful to have the bank to draft a certain amount of their wages and allocate it to their savings account each month.

How much should you save? It depends on your circumstances. A good guide is to strive to save what you can afford. Many family economists recommend maintaining a savings that is equal to two months of salary earnings. Some couples save a set amount ($100 or $50 each month) while others save a percentage (10%, for example) each pay day.

Develop a Financial Plan

"The action that most helped us get our finances in order was making a financial plan," said Alice. "We identified our long-range goals, like starting our own business in five years and a college education for the children and our short-range goals, like taking a vacation or buying a new car."

Once the goals are agreed upon, decisions are made on a daily basis to achieve those goals. Strategies need to be planned and implemented which will help you accomplish your goals, such as setting aside a certain amount of money each month to invest in starting the family business or in the children's college education fund.

Use Credit Properly

Few things cause the misuse of credit or contribute to financial problems faster than the indiscriminate use of credit cards.

"Our credit card debt nearly destroyed us financially," shared Ruth. "We had four different cards and we were using credit card purchases to live beyond our means. We didn't keep receipts or records of our credit card purchases. We could only manage to pay the minimum payment most of the time.

"It took us years to get this under control," she observed. "We consolidated our credit card debts and destroyed all the credit cards except one which we only use occasionally or for emergencies. We also began to keep a record of the total amount that we owed on the credit card at any one time."

Many people share Ruth's experience with credit card debt. The interest or finance charge on many cards is 22% annually. If only the minimum monthly payment is made, a moderately large credit card debt is simply not reduced. Minimum payments may barely pay the interest charges, so it can take a very long time to pay off a credit debt of $2,000 or more. If payments are late, late charges are very high. It is possible to have the balance increase even though minimum payments are made just a few days late!

Couples who are successful in managing their finances have found certain strategies to be helpful in using credit wisely.

- **Commit yourself to a lower level of living until a significant reduction in your debt level has been achieved.** This is difficult for anyone to do. But the adjustment is easier if we recognize that this sacrifice is temporary and that we are making real progress toward solvency.

- **Set a ceiling for your credit debts.** A good guide suggested by several financial consultants is to limit the total of your credit debt to 15-20% of your take home pay. This should include all credit debts except your mortgage payments.

- **Limit your credit card charges to what you can pay off within 30 days.** "This is a very helpful technique that helps us stay ahead of our credit card debts," shares an Indiana husband. "When we are considering a credit card purchase we ask ourselves if we can pay the purchase off within 30 days. If the answer is yes, we often put it on the credit card. If the answer is no, we do not make the credit card purchase."

- **Keep a record of all credit purchases.** It is important to keep receipts as a record and always to maintain an accurate running total of your credit purchases so that you know how much you owe. This practice helps to keep from accumulating debts larger than you can manage.

- **Realize that it is not a good idea to use credit to live beyond your means, for impulse buying, or to meet day-to-day living expenses.** If you find yourself consistently using credit for any of these purposes it should be a red flag that you are using credit unwisely.

- **Be aware that there are instances when it may be wise to use credit.** For example it may be desirable to use credit to avoid price increases. This is particularly true for major items that can be purchased on sale.

You may wish to use credit when it is interest free. Sometimes items can be purchased on credit with no interest charges for the first three or six months. If you can pay off the balance in the no-interest time this can be a wise way to use credit. Also, if you buy something on October 4 on a credit card for which billing is October 5, the charge will not show up on your bill until the November statement. This allows a month of no-interest use of the money.

Another good time to use credit is when you know you will be reimbursed for the bills. For example, you may use your credit card to pay for a hospital bill. You probably will have received reimbursement from your insurance company by the time the charge clears the credit card company and comes back to you. Therefore, it will not be necessary for you to pay any interest charges. However, when using credit in any of these ways, you must be meticulous about paying off the balance before interest is charged. Otherwise, there is no benefit. Be sure to read the fine print to understand the terms exactly.

Use a Budget to Achieve Goals and Manage Resources

A simple monthly budget can help you to be more successful in following the other principles of good financial management: directing the cash flow, developing a financial plan, and using credit properly.

A budget should be a flexible guide. It should not enslave you. Your budget needs to allow for seasonal fluctuations in certain expenses. For example, expenditures for gifts will be greatest during the Christmas season and clothing expenditures may be highest in

August and September because of getting children outfitted for school.

"We kept a record of our expenses for three months and then created our monthly budget," reported Deborah. "This took a lot of time but it gave us an accurate idea of where our money was going." Deborah's practice is helpful in developing a realistic budget.

The following budget may serve as a helpful model.

Monthly Budget

Income
> Monthly take-home income   _____

Money Set Aside for Savings and Investment
> Monthly allocation for temporary savings   _____
> Monthly allocation for
> > long-term investment   _____

Fixed Expenses (Those That Remain Constant)
> Car payments   _____
> Insurance premiums   _____
> Rent or house payments   _____
> Utilities   _____
> Other debt payments (credit card, loans)   _____

Variable (Those That Are Irregular or Discretionary)
> Food   _____
> Entertainment/travel   _____
> Clothing   _____
> Automobile upkeep   _____
> Health care   _____
> Church/charity contributions   _____
> Gifts   _____

Before putting your budget into operation, you and your spouse should discuss some basic questions. Is the budget realistic? Does it provide for major long-range and short-range goals? Does the budget allow for the possibility of emergencies? Does it permit you to live within your income? Many software packages have financial planning and/or budget sheets. Several web sites have financial information.

Make Financial Management Part of Your Total Relationship

Couples argue about money more than any other single topic. The three major issues that couples argue about are: deciding what to spend money on, spending beyond budget limits, and the price to pay for things.

It is easy to disagree about money because money is tangible and part of everyday life. For most of us, money is limited, and consequently, we have to decide how and when and how much to spend. Conflict over finances also happens because other issues such as a power struggle or feelings of not being appreciated are involved in decisions about the use of money.

It is not surprising that a husband and wife will probably wish to spend money differently. The way a person manages money will be influenced by personality and temperament, past experiences, and interests. We are each different and we must understand and respect those differences in order to resolve financial conflicts and to integrate financial management successfully into the total marriage relationship.

"Our most fierce quarrels have been over money," said Ramone. "I came from a family where my father made all of the financial decisions even to telling my mother how much to spend on groceries each week."

Ramone's wife, Marie, came from a family where her mother had shared in making economic decisions. No wonder they clashed.

"Ramone would get furious when I disagreed with his decisions," added Marie. "He thought I was questioning his leadership. I guess I got angry because I felt he was not respecting my feelings or my ability to make decisions."

Ramone and Marie eventually worked through their differences. They continue to keep lines of communication open because they value their marriage relationship. As a result they have come to understand the underlying factors contributing to their quarrels over money. Furthermore, they have been able to respect differences and work out ways to manage their finances that are effective for them.

HOW TO LOVE YOUR IN-LAWS

An old bit of folk wisdom says that when a couple get married there are really six people getting married; the bride and her mother and father, and the groom and his mother and father. Some do not understand the truth of this statement. "I don't care for his parents. But it doesn't matter because I am marrying him, not his family," argued Jennifer, a college student. Unfortunately her attitude is inaccurate. It does matter. In many ways, Jennifer is getting married to his family as well as to him. His parents have had a great influence upon him and have played a great role in who he is as a person. His family cannot be ignored because he needs to continue to have a relationship with them. Furthermore, Jennifer cannot avoid having some sort of relationship with his family. It will be better for her marriage if it is a positive relationship. Having a close relationship with your spouse's parents can also help you to understand how your spouse became the person you know and love.

The kind of person each of us becomes is largely the result of the genes we inherited from our parents and of the variety of influences we have experienced as we have matured. The lifestyle we have chosen; the foods we eat; the books we read; our religious attitudes; our views on sex, marriage, friendship, and how men and women should treat each other are all influenced by our parents.

The statement that in-law relationships are important to the well-being of a marriage is underscored by the fact that those couples who have a high degree of marriage satisfaction are likely to have good relationships with their in-laws. When the relationships are good, in-laws can be a great asset and support for your marriage. If relationships are bad, in-laws can be a constant stress and strain on your marriage.

One husband stated, "I have a very close relationship with Jill's parents. One reason we get along so well is that I have always known how important they are to her. I didn't expect her to stop seeing them just because we got married.

"Financial problems forced us to live with them in our third year of marriage. It gave me an opportunity to know them on an everyday basis. And I realized that so many of the good qualities I love in Jill came from her parents. Her marvelous wit is from her father; her optimism and enthusiasm, from her mother."

WHAT ARE THE PROBLEMS?

Years ago Dr. Evelyn Duval did a classic study of in-law relationships in which she identified the most common complaints against children-in-law and the most common complaints against parents-in-law. Similar findings have been discovered in our research and in the research of others. Below is a listing of the major complaints against parents-in-law (made from the perspective of the children-in-law) and the major complaints against children-in-law (made from the perspective of the parents-in-law).[3]

Major Complaints Against Parents-in-law	Major Complaints Against Children-in-law
Meddlesome	Indifferent
Nagging	Distant
Criticizing	Thoughtless
Possessive	Inconsiderate
Aloof	Too busy to be interested in parents' lives

"They always give us advice we haven't asked for," complains one young husband. "It gets tiresome. It makes us feel like they don't think we are capable of making our own decisions." However, often underlying the problem behavior of parents-in-law is a genuine concern for their child and son-in-law or daughter-in-law. The difficulties arise because parents have a hard time NOT giving advice and information to their child and his/her spouse. After all, the parents have years of experience and "know now" coupled with a desire to help the children. Concern for a child doesn't just stop at his/her wedding. Unfortunately concern may come across as meddling or nagging.

It is also true that much of the problem behavior of children-in-law is actually a reflection of their attempts to establish their "own family." Newly married couples do need to devote most of their time and attention to each other. They do need to be independent. Unfortunately, the children-in-law may seem distant, indifferent, or too busy to spend time with the parents-in-law.

Most conflict with in-laws involves the women in the family. In fact, more conflict occurs between the mother-in-law and the daughter-in-law than anyone else. The major reason for greater amounts of conflict between mother-in-law and daughter-in-law is that they are most similar in their roles. Both are likely to be heavily involved in the management of the household and the rearing of children. Frequently those roles are openly available for comparison.

A simple backyard family cookout, for example, presents a number of opportunities for comparisons which may lead to comments or suggestions and conflict:

"Does my son look healthy or too tired?"

"Did she plan a nice meal?"

"Are they using too much salt with their meals?"

"Are the children well behaved?"

"Do the house and yard look tidy?"

In contrast, fewer male roles are openly available for comparison. The son-in-law and father-in-law rarely are employed in the same profession and most likely don't work together even if they are. How each fulfills his occupational role is not easily observed by the other.

Also, neither the father-in-law nor the son-in-law is likely to be as heavily involved in parental or household roles as the mother-in-law and daughter-in-law.

Of course, other factors contribute to the conflict between mother-in-law and daughter-in-law. While they perform many of the same roles that are openly comparable, they almost certainly have learned to do them differently because they come from different family cultures and from different generations.

Certainly, conflict is more likely to occur when different methods and preferences are judged inferior just because they are different. Often, when this happens, underlying messages of disrespect and criticism are communicated, causing hurt feelings and resentment.

Personal immaturity plays a large role in conflict. This is often the case when the daughter-in-law is extremely sensitive about her autonomy and interprets any constructive suggestions as meddling.

Sometimes conflict is caused because the mother-in-law feels that she has lost her son to the daughter-in-law. This feeling is not always simply due to the mother-in-law's inability to make appropriate adjustments to the fact that her son now has his own family. Some evidence suggest that couples tend to spend substantially more time visiting with the wife's family than they do with the husband's family. When this happens, it is easy to see how this could cause parents to feel rejected and to begin to resent the daughter-in-law.

BUILDING GOOD IN-LAW RELATIONSHIPS

Because in-laws are people, some disagreements are bound to happen. However, serious conflict with in-laws is not inevitable; relationships do not have to be destroyed. Quite the contrary, many couples experience very positive relationships with their in-laws. There are five principles for building good in-law relationships which many happily married couples have found to be very important.

Be Realistic but Optimistic

It is important to be realistic in the sense of recognizing that no one is perfect – not your in-laws and not you. Each of you will make mistakes. Once you have accepted that, why be outraged when imperfections emerge?

It is also equally important to be optimistic. Remember that many people experience satisfying in-law relationships and so can you. Don't approach your relationships with negative stereotypes and with an attitude of expecting the worst. When you do this, you can bring about a self-fulfilling prophecy. If you expect your in-laws to be a pain, your behavior may reflect that attitude. For example, if you expect them to be meddlesome, you may interpret every question or suggestion (even innocent, ordinary ones) as meddling. You may be aloof and defensive or irritable with them. They, in turn, may be hurt or confused by your reactions and may become negative toward you.

Focus on Strengths and Accept Differences

Ralph and Sally are typical of the many couples who enjoy positive relationships with in-laws. As Sally shares, "Ralph's mother and I are about as different as any two people could be concerning our political beliefs. She is extremely conservative and I guess I am extremely liberal.

"I probably don't keep house clean enough to suit her and we have different philosophies about childrearing," continued Sally. "But the surprising thing is we like each other and have a very good relationship. The reason is we respect each other's differences.

"I think the key for me was when I learned not to react or argue when she pointed out the error of my political positions or suggested different childrearing methods," explained Sally. "Instead I hear her out. I don't have to change my thinking – or hers. I don't concentrate on what she did that irritated me; I choose to think about her strong points and the things about her that I do like. For example, she is extremely well read and up-to-date on anything political that is going on. I do enjoy talking with her. I think she does the same with me."

Avoid Conflict Over the Trivial or What Cannot Be Changed

Most in-law conflict is over trivial issues or things that cannot be changed. Any couple can take a giant step toward building more satisfying in-law relationships by following this principle.

Ask yourself if the issue of disagreement is a truly important matter. If it involves differences over lifestyle matters such as mealtimes, music, or style of furniture, it probably isn't worth a battle. Change the subject or politely suggest that you just don't agree and do not argue.

"Nothing I say or do is going to change my son-in-law's political views so it's silly for me to try," said a Michigan man. "I am not going to ruin our relationship by arguing with him all the time about something that's not going to change. And in the grand scheme of things it's not that important either."

Learn to Reframe

"I can't stand her," said one New Mexico woman of her mother-in-law. "She meddles in every aspect of our lives and drives me crazy."

Dissatisfaction with in-laws is amplified when we become hypnotized by a particular quality that we don't like in an in-law. We focus on it and emphasize that disliked quality until it multiplies in importance.

This self-hypnosis also makes it difficult for us to see the good qualities in that person. In a sense, it programs us to become irritable and confrontational. We expect problems and that leads us to respond in more negative ways to the person, actually bringing about problems in the relationship. Our expectations bring about a self-fulfilling prophecy.

We will experience more successful in-law relationships and also be happier individuals if we model what many of the happily married couples in our research reported doing – reframing! They said it in different ways, but basically reframing involves taking a disliked quality and deliberately taking a positive perspective on it. It is a bit of mental gymnastics.

Cathy, a New England wife, describes how she used the reframing method.

"My father-in-law is not an easy person to get along with," she said. "He thought we were too permissive with the children.

"This hurt my feelings and made me angry," she shared. "I knew I could not continue to feel this way and ever hope to have a good relationship with him.

"What helped me to turn this around was realizing that what I did not like in him – his strict discipline – was an extreme form of a good quality. He wanted the children to turn out well; he wanted them to avoid experiencing major problems in the future."

"When I was able to look at him in this way it helped me to feel less defensive and to feel more positive toward him," she said. "I was able to make my responses more positive and to enjoy our relationship more."

Consider the following as examples of how you can reframe:

This Disliked Quality	is an extreme expression of	This Positive Quality
Meddlesome		Concerned
Stingy		Thrifty
Bossy		Shows leadership
Rigid		Organized
Chaotic		Flexible/creative
Critical		Wants to make things better and avoid problems
Rebellious		Independent

Expand Your Concept of Family

No principle is more important than this one for developing good in-law relationships. A Tennessee husband reflects an attitude that is typical of many of the happily married couples in our research.

"I really consider my wife's parents as my parents also," he said. "I don't look at them as my in-laws but rather as my second set of parents.

"I spent time with them and got to know them pretty well before we got married. The relationship just grew from that point."

Heather, a South Carolina wife, shares a similar view. "Because my husband's parents are a very important part of his life I knew that I needed to have a good relationship with them.

"I discovered that when I referred to them as my in-laws, it sort of put a barrier between me and them in my own mind. When I thought of them as part of my family I felt closer to them," she shared.

"What really made this clear to me was reading the story of Tobit in the Catholic Bible," she said. "At the end of the wedding celebration for Tobiah and Sarah, the father of Sarah kissed her and said, 'My daughter, honor your father-in-law and your mother-in-law, because from now on they are as much your parents as the ones who brought you into the world.' That is a powerful message. I have made a point of looking at my mother-in-law and my father-in-law as my parents. I think it has helped me to be kinder and more loving toward them."

Expand your concept of family to include your in-laws. As you do this, it will help you to become more tolerant of their imperfections. It will also encourage you to be more positive in your responses toward them.

Chapter 7

NAVIGATING DANGEROUS WATERS:
How Couples Overcome Addictions
How to "Affair Proof" Your Marriage

As mentioned in the previous chapter, life isn't like a fairy tale or romance novel and married couples are going to experience some difficult times. Finances and in-law relationships were discussed earlier as two rough spots that affect almost all married couples – to some degree at some point in their marriage.

Two other areas of threat to a marriage relationship are addictions and extramarital sexual relationships (affairs). Your first reaction may be that these are not going to happen in a successful marriage. Remember that people in successful marriages encounter hazardous circumstances and they make mistakes, too. The difference is that they find ways to navigate safely through those dangerous waters.

HOW COUPLES OVERCOME ADDICTIONS

At the mention of addiction, most people think of dependence on alcohol or an illegal drug such as cocaine. Many will also immediately think that an addiction is a problem that belongs to someone else who lives far away. In reality, addiction is a problem that is close to many of us.

If we consider problems of abuse and dependence on illicit drugs, about 1 in 25 adults in America is involved. For alcohol problems the number increases to 1 in 10 American adults. That means that the chances are good that may of us will be affected – directly or indirectly – by drug or alcohol addiction.

If we expand our thinking on addiction to include other forms of dependence and/or misuse (such as food, gambling, pornography, prescription drugs, sex, work, television, and computers), the numbers of persons affected increases dramatically. Of course, addiction to heroin or gambling is not the same in many ways as addiction to television. Nevertheless, even though there are different kinds of addictions, they all pose a threat to a healthy, happy marriage. Some are quite deadly threats.

WHAT ADDICTIONS HAVE IN COMMON

All addictions share certain characteristics which interfere with healthy marriage relationships. First, whatever the addiction it becomes all absorbing and all consuming. The affected person loses interest in anything that does not include the addiction. His or her energies, time, and money are used up in finding drugs, a sex partner or porno magazine, or in traveling to the casino. Addicted persons also lose a sense of control and – regardless of the nature of the addiction – it is truly bondage for them and their families. As a result, the addicted person – and family members – recognize that the addiction is causing problems in their lives.

Other characteristics that addicted persons may manifest include:

- Feelings of stress, anxiety, and guilt
- Taking unreasonable risks
- Paranoia
- Undermining family unity
- Setting a bad example for their children
- Feelings of loneliness and isolation
- Poor self-esteem
- Feelings of enslavement
- Excessive emotionality that interferes with daily functions
- Feeling that everything is out of control
- Sense of helplessness and hopelessness
- Depression

HOW ADDICTIONS HURT MARRIAGE RELATIONSHIPS

Addictions undermine a marriage relationship in four major ways. First, the addiction takes priority over the marriage in the life of the affected person. A spouse and the marriage relationship take a back seat to work, lottery tickets, a porno film, another drink, or some pills. Nothing and no one is more important in the addict's life.

The second way that an addiction undermines the marriage relationship is directly related to the first. The addiction consumes the affected person's time, energy, thoughts, and resources. As a result, less and less time is invested in the marriage relationship. This naturally leaves a spouse feeling neglected, unloved, hurt, and resentful.

A third way an addiction hurts the marriage relationship is by creating a great deal of stress.[1] Much stress may be produced by the financial strain caused by the expense of supporting the addiction.

Drug dependence, alcoholism and gambling, in particular, can spiral a couple into bankruptcy. The addicted person's absence from home can cause anxiety and worry over his or her safety. Has he been arrested? Is she driving under the influence? The excessive emotionality of the addicted spouse – extreme anger, paranoia, and depression – increases the emotional stress in the marriage relationship. Conflict situations occur often and may be highly charged.

A fourth way that an addiction erodes the marriage relationship is by destroying the trust between spouses. The secrecy and deceit involved in maintaining an addiction often result in the addicted person lying to his or her partner. The deceit and lying can become so persuasive that a spouse may not believe the addicted partner about anything.

George, for example, is an alcoholic. His abusive drinking started in high school with friends who drank and partied. George came to associate having a good time with drinking to the point of getting drunk. Now in his late 20's, he no longer has control over his drinking. He often starts out by intending to have just a couple of drinks but ends up having another and another until he is in a drunken stupor.

George typically begins a drinking binge on Friday evening with his friends and continues until Sunday afternoon or night. He has difficulty getting up for work on Monday morning so he often calls in sick. Over the years his drinking has gradually extended into the work week. Although he usually does not binge during the week, he often has a hangover and is late for work.

Before Rhoda and George married she thought his drinking was just a part of having a good time at social gatherings since most of their friends also drank. She was not aware of how his alcohol dependence and abuse would grow.

During the five years she and George have been married she has seen his drinking progress to the point where he is in serious danger of losing his job. She has also watched a disturbing increase in his emotional instability. George has grown more irritable and goes through extreme mood swings of depression and anger.

George's behavior has become increasingly erratic and unpredictable. Just recently he pushed and slapped Rhoda during a disagreement.

Because she is concerned about her safety, Rhoda has left George and is staying with a friend temporarily. She is torn between her desire to save her marriage and help George recover, and her growing doubt about their future together.

COUPLES WHO OVERCOME ADDICTIONS

The case of Rhoda and George helps us to see some of the reasons why the divorce rate is high among couples where one has an addiction. Addictive behavior causes much frustration and pain in a relationship. But it is important to know that there are couples who have overcome serious addiction and built strong, successful marriages out of the depths of despair. We know this is true because we have met some of those couples in our research.

Consider the example of Bill and Rita. They had been married seven years when they became aware that Rita was addicted to pain pills. She had begun the use of pain pills because of a neck injury received in a car accident. However, she had continued to use the medication long after her injury had healed. At first it wasn't hard: She would tell her physician that her neck still bothered her and have her prescription renewed.

In reality, Rita had become very dependent on these prescription drugs even though she wasn't aware of it. Bill became concerned because Rita was behaving in ways that she would never have behaved earlier. She would pick fights. She was arrogant and hostile. Rita perceived meanings in people's comments that were not intended. She often felt that others were against her and intended to do things to embarrass or hurt her.

Rita experienced periods of severe anxiety. She was often depressed and frequently had suicidal thoughts. Her sleep patterns were disturbed making it hard to sleep at night. Consequently she slept more in the day and the household and children were being neglected. Because of Bill's concern, she checked into a residential treatment program. A model patient, she was home in a month. Rita was free of medication for several months before a woman in her exercise class offered her something for her aching muscles. Rita was caught up in craving again. This time her physician would not prescribe for her so she sought out another source.

She met her supplier of illegal prescription medicine at a nearby casino. It was a good place to meet and Rita enjoyed the atmosphere of the casino. The flashing lights and ringing bells suggested that someone was always winning lots of money. She tried the slots and won enough to keep her coming back; she moved on to games with higher stakes.

Before long Rita was visiting the casino between meetings with her pill supplier. Her gambling habit had begun in an attempt to bring some sense of recreation, adventure, social contact, and even meaning to her life. The result was financial disaster. The combination of the money spent on drugs and the accumulation of gambling debts created a financial crisis.

Shortly after this crisis point, Rita entered a residential rehabilitation program for the second time. This time she stayed three months. Getting her to go into the program was very difficult, but Rita gradually began to respond favorably to treatment. This was the beginning of the real healing process and over the following months and years her physical, emotional, intellectual, social, and spiritual life improved.

During the years of her addiction and treatment, there were very difficult times for Rita and Bill. Some friends and relatives encouraged Bill to divorce Rita. On a few occasions even the children told Bill they would be better off without their mother. But Bill did not divorce Rita, and he did not give up on her.

Twenty years after the addiction problems began, Rita has recovered and is doing well. Not only has their marriage survived, but it has grown strong and close. How did Bill and Rita overcome the addiction problems?

HOW SUCCESSFUL COUPLES HAVE
OVERCOME ADDICTION

The secrets to the success of Rita and Bill and the other couples who have overcome the pain and frustration of different types of addiction are the same. First, the affected person must come to want to change. That desire to change typically comes as a result of a crisis – a low point for the person and family. It may include financial loss, illness, arrest or legal troubles, and/or pressure from family members. Then the addicted person gets needed help through professional assistance, support groups, and the positive influence of good friends and family.

Second, the non-addicted partner plays a very important role. What did Bill and other non-addicted spouses do to deal successfully with the marriage-threatening problem of addiction? The successful couples who have overcome the problem of addiction report the following principles to be most important.

Act with Maturity

The non-addicted partner must possess a high degree of emotional maturity. This is vital because an addiction tends to magnify immature behavior in the addicted person. If both partners are behaving immaturely the strain on the marriage will be increased, and there will be less likelihood the couple will be able to overcome the addiction. One member of the couple must be able to demonstrate high levels of patience, kindness, support, and rationality.

Practice Unselfishness

"Bill reached out to me and without that I never would have made it," said Rita. "He sacrificed a lot for me. I know he went through hell. At any time he could have decided he had suffered enough and left. But he didn't and I believe his ability to be unselfish during all those times when I was difficult and causing everyone so much pain probably saved our marriage."

Set Boundaries

It is also necessary to set boundaries to let the addicted spouse know clearly what is not acceptable and will not be tolerated. Limits provide a healthy balance to the support, patience, and kindness being shown to the addicted spouse. Without boundaries, the non-addicted spouse may get tricked into enabling (helping) the person to remain addicted. One wife reported, "I told my husband that I loved him and would do everything possible for him to get free of his drug addiction. But I told him that one thing I would not tolerate anymore was being physically abused by him. I told him if it ever happened again I was leaving and our marriage would be over. He never hit me again. I think in some way this helped him with the recovery process."

Bill shares a similar story. "I let Rita know that we would get through this thing together and I would be with her every step of the way. But I could not deal with the overwhelming burden of any more gambling debts. When Rita stopped going to the casino it helped our financial survival but it was also a big step in her drug rehabilitation since her drug supplier had been meeting her in the casino."

Don't Abandon

"He never gave up on me," mused Rita. "That meant everything. I don't think I would be alive today if he had given up on me and left, because I had given up on myself." Persons who are struggling with an addiction often feel lonely and isolated, hopeless, and unworthy. This is why the continuing support, encouragement, and caring provided by the non-addicted spouse are so critical to both the well-being of the addicted spouse and the marriage.

Maintain High Self-Esteem

It is important for the non-addicted spouse to nurture his or her own self-esteem in order to stay a positive force in the marriage and in the recovery of the addicted person. "Don't let the addiction destroy the way you feel about yourself," said Bill. "It is easy to get discouraged because the healing process in an addiction is slow. But if you become depressed and feel bad about yourself that will not be a help to your addicted spouse or the marriage.

"Be good to yourself," advised Bill. "Make a point to do things that will boost your self-confidence. Count your blessings. Spend time everyday thinking about your past successes. Don't dwell on setbacks or failures. Doing these things will help protect you from feeling bad about yourself."

Maintain a Good Image of the Addicted Spouse

How we see ourselves is determined in part by how we think others see us. Each of us needs someone in our life who can see our potential and not form judgments of us that are limited to our past or by our mistakes.

"Bill always saw the part of me that could rise above the pills and gambling," said Rita. "He would say to me, 'This addiction is not all of who you are; it does not define who you are.' He always saw the lovely part of me even when I was not lovely. I think this helped give me some confidence that my life could be different."

This seems to be a key principle in preventing an addiction from destroying a marriage and in helping the addicted spouse in the recovery process. It is very important that the non-addicted spouse make a conscious effort to see the good qualities and the potential in the addicted spouse and to show that image of good and positive qualities to the recovering spouse. This helps both persons to feel hopeful and positive; it boosts everyone's self esteem.

Have Determination

"I think just making the decision that you are going to get through the addiction and that you are not going to let it defeat you generates a kind of power that helps you and your partner," said Bill. The couples who overcame addictions were fortified by a steel-like determination that helps them to weather the stress, pain, and disappointment that are part of addictions. It helps the couple to look beyond the addiction problems and to stay focused on the goal of recovery.

Be Good Problem Solvers

One common theme that is clearly visible among the couples who have successfully overcome addiction is that they are good problem solvers. Instead of blaming each other or becoming hypnotized by the pain they are experiencing, they stay focused on dealing effectively with the problem (addiction).

"I kept reminding myself and Rita that the addiction was not the real Rita and that we needed to put our efforts into getting her well," said Bill.

Simply being aware of all the different options they have at their disposal is a very critical part of being good problem solvers. "Sometimes you need to do a lot of homework to find out what your options are," observed Bill. "Then when you know the options you can evaluate them and make a better decision."

Many couples who have overcome addiction have shared the importance of continuing to look for the answers. Their successful problem solving involves a persistent search for the best treatment and an enduring quest for how they can best remove stumbling blocks and stress.

Find Support

Lonnie did not know where to turn. He could not face his wife. He didn't have any friends. He did what he felt was his last hope. He walked into church on a Sunday evening. It was the church his parents attended and the church he used to attend, although he had not been there in over two years.

He poured out his problem to the minister. With Lonnie's consent, the minister shared the situation with the congregation that night and a special prayer was offered for Lonnie. The result was an outpouring of caring and support that became a turning point in his life.

When Lonnie walked into the church that night he was 28 years old and had been battling cocaine addiction for years. The previous day he had experienced a relapse and had spent his entire paycheck on a purchase of cocaine. There was no money left to pay the bills or buy food. His young son was sick, but there was not enough money to take him to the doctor.

"If I had not turned to this church I would be in the grave," said Lonnie. The loving, caring people of the church opened their hearts to Lonnie and formed a source of support to him at a time when help was not found anywhere else.

"This will put a great strain on my marriage. I don't know if our marriage will survive this," Lonnie had said that night.

The marriage was strained but it survived. They received counseling and later participated in a marriage enrichment program. Not only did the marriage survive, it also was healed of its wounds.

Lonnie went through another drug rehabilitation program. This program was different from others in that it had a greater spiritual emphasis which Lonnie felt was important for him. He and his wife became actively involved in their church which continues to be a major source of support for their entire family.

Most couples who overcome addiction report that a good network of support is vital in their recovery. Couples find the support in different places. For Lonnie the most meaningful support at that point in his life was a church filled with loving, caring people. For others it might be in friends or family members.

Generally the cases given in this discussion of addictions have dealt with problems of addiction to drugs, alcohol, or gambling. Most would agree that the nature of addiction in certain areas such as these and sex and pornography are more difficult than other addictions. However, any addiction – even to soap operas or golf – can interfere with a satisfactory marriage relationship, and some addictions such as to work or to shopping can pose significant threats to a marriage even though there isn't anything basically wrong with the activity. Consequently all addictions should be taken seriously.

HOW TO "AFFAIR PROOF" YOUR MARRIAGE

When we consider all of the situations that can destroy a marriage, probably nothing poses a greater threat than an extramarital sexual relationship – an affair. Affairs play an important role in contributing to divorce.[2] Some research indicates that over a third of couples eventually divorce as a direct result of their extramarital sexual relationships. Some estimates suggest that the majority of divorces are, in fact, caused by adultery regardless of the legal cause reported.

Dean and Sara have enjoyed a happy marriage of eleven years. Their marriage relationship has many strengths – they have good communication and mutual respect and they enjoy doing many things together. All of this was recently jeopardized by an affair Dean had been involved in for the past few months.

Dean's job responsibilities required that he work closely with a woman he found attractive. The feeling was mutual. She flirted with Dean and let him know she was attracted to him. Dean was quite flattered by her attention to him and gradually found himself drawn into a pattern of seductive courtship. Soon they were involved in an intense affair that everyone at work knew about.

Sara received a call from a friend who worked in the same office complex with Dean telling her about the affair. Shocked and very upset, she confronted Dean. At first he denied it but later he admitted everything to her.

Dean was devastated when he realized how deeply Sara was hurt by his actions. Immediately he had terminated the affair. He assured Sara that he loved her and that their marriage was more important to him than anything else. He begged her to forgive him and not to leave him. Sara had difficulty believing him. She told him she couldn't trust him anymore and wasn't sure she wanted to live with him any longer.

It is not uncommon for a couple with a good marriage, like Dean and Sara, to have the marriage threatened and perhaps destroyed by an affair. Why do individuals such as Dean become involved in affairs?

REASONS FOR AFFAIRS

There are a number of circumstances that influence people to have affairs. Awareness of these circumstances can increase our understanding of affairs. This awareness can also be an aid to a couple in affair proofing their marriage since each of the reasons reflects needs that can be more effectively met in ways other than marital infidelity.

Social Encouragement

Some people engage in extramarital relationships because of pressure to do so in various social situations. For example, at some business parties, sexual involvements are expected, and some otherwise monogamous husbands and wives participate in extramarital sexual activities at these times. Some evidence indicates that a substantial percentage (about 40%) of people who have been involved in extramarital sexual relationships have reported that the critical influences were the places and people that presented opportunities for liaisons.

Curiosity

Some individuals enter an extramarital sexual relationship primarily out of curiosity to find out what it would be like to have a sexual encounter with someone other than a spouse. "I wanted sexual variety," stated one man. "That is the main reason I have had affairs."

Escape from Boredom

One basic reason given by many persons for engaging in affairs is to escape boredom. Many people who feel that they lead highly routinized, dull, unadventureous lives, both at home and at work, see an affair as one of the few ways they can experience excitement and adventure.

Increase Self-Esteem

An affair is often an attempt to reinforce a good feeling about oneself and to feel desirable and attractive more than it is to experience physical pleasure. Many men and women do not feel good about themselves. They feel inadequate or too old or too plump. They have nagging doubts concerning themselves and believe they are not really masculine or feminine unless they continually win the attentions and romantic interests of others. When someone flirts or indicates an attraction, the boost to self-esteem is tremendously hard to resist.

Avoidance of Problems

A husband or wife who is having problems with a job, finances, or a mate may try to forget them for a little while in the companionship of another person. People may also use the extramarital relationship as a way to create other problems that can, in a sense, be substituted for those they wish to avoid.

Breakdowns in the Marriage Relationship

"I can't ever talk with my husband," said Doris. "He is a workaholic and he is gone a lot. When he is here he gives me the impression that he is just too busy to listen to me. In other words I'm not important enough.

"I have grown to resent him for making me feel this way," she explained. "And I have stopped trying and we have just drifted further apart.

"About six months ago I began having an affair with a man at work," Doris shared. "He is kind. I felt comfortable talking with him. At first we were just good friends. Our friendship developed into something more serious, however.

"This has turned my life upside down," she said. "My friends know about the affair. People at work know. I live in dread of when my husband finds out. Maybe he already knows.

"I don't think I want my marriage to end," Doris added. "I would like for us to change some things about our marriage but I don't know if it can survive this situation."

Many people like Doris become involved in extramarital relationships because of breakdowns in their marriage relationships. They may drift apart as Doris and her husband did. Or a couple may find their incompatibility growing and conflict becoming a continuous experience. And this may prompt an affair.

Retaliation

In some situations the major motivation for becoming involved in an affair is not sexual interest in another person but to "get even" and to hurt a spouse for some "wrong" he or she has committed.

Gabe and Sandy have been married for six years. They have found themselves involved in more frequent conflict during the last two years. Sandy's income is higher than Gabe's and because of that she insists she should make most of the decisions about how the money is spent.

Another area of conflict is that when Gabe comes in from work, Sandy usually has a list of chores she wants him to do. If he wants to spend his time in another way, she gets angry and insists that he should do his "fair share."

Gabe usually gives in to Sandy, but he is angry about it and resents her attitude. Gabe has started an affair with an attractive young woman. He has made no attempt to keep his wife from knowing about it. He wants her to know. He wants to hurt Sandy. The affair is his revenge for the dominating way she has treated him.

Search for Emotional Intimacy

"I became involved with Patty about a year ago," said Al. My wife found out about two months ago. She is very upset.

"I'm sorry she found out. I don't want to hurt my wife," said Al. "But I don't want to hurt Patty either. She is such a sweet person and I feel very protective toward her. I want to take care of her and nurture her. I think that's what attracted me to her. I could never seem to have that with my wife. She is too self-sufficient."

Some who engage in extramarital relationships are seeking to have certain emotional needs satisfied. These needs may be unfulfilled within the marriage relationship, or there may be a desire to expand emotional intimacy to persons outside of the marriage.

Desire to Destroy Relationships

James found himself very attracted to a new neighbor, Beth, who had shown a lot of interest in him since she moved into the neighborhood. James and Beth soon became involved in a tumultuous affair that eventually destroyed his ten-year marriage.

Shortly after the divorce was finalized, Beth ended the relationship. James was stunned. After all, he had given up his marriage and family for Beth. Now she had ended their relationship which he had assumed would develop into a new marriage. James was very confused.

Some individuals, because they do not feel good about themselves, have an unconscious or conscious desire to destroy relationships. These persons sometimes base their lives on the assumption that good relationships do not exist and their behavior is directed toward "proving" this assumption.

One illustration of this is, as in the case of Beth and James, when an individual establishes an extramarital relationship that "just happens" to break up the extramarital partner's marriage. After the marriage has been destroyed, the affair itself "just happens" to break up. The individual with this destructive orientation toward relationships has structured the situation in a way that "proves" that the other person's marriage relationship was not good and neither was the extramarital relationship. This type of person is expressing an "I don't feel good about myself and you are not much good either" approach to relationships.

THE EFFECTS OF AFFAIRS

One important consequence of an extramarital sexual relationship is that it minimizes the enjoyment of the positive qualities of the spouse. World-renowned sex researchers, William Masters and Virginia Johnson, observed that extramarital affairs communicate two destructive messages from the spouse who is engaged in the affair to his or her marriage partner. The first hurtful message is: "You are not capable of meeting my emotional and physical needs." The second message is: "You are not a unique and irreplaceable source of sexual satisfaction." The effect of these messages is to reduce self-esteem, self-confidence, and security in the spouse who receives them. Persons who are loyal to a spouse and restrict sexual expression to the marriage partner learn to look more deeply into the positive qualities possessed by a spouse.

John has been having an affair for four months. During this time he has experienced stomach problems and digestive disturbances. He has difficulty sleeping and is bothered by nightmares. He has become forgetful and is increasingly unable to concentrate on his work. His friends have noticed that he is more irritable and moody.

Affairs often cause intense feelings of conflict within the individual between a desire to maintain the marriage and a desire to continue the affair. The more open an individual is to the affair, the more that person is pressured to shut out the marriage relationship. The more a person seeks to preserve the marriage the more it becomes necessary to terminate the extramarital relationship. Many people in this situation find they can end the dilemma only by choosing one relationship and abandoning the other.

One influence that determines how much internal conflict an affair causes is the personality of the individual. For example, for conscience-controlled people who had or desired to have a totally involved and committed marriage, it is very likely that there will be a great deal of internal conflict over an affair.

For this personality type the affair tends to be a disruptive and dynamic experience that either grows at the expense of the marriage or is diminished or terminated in favor of the marriage. Consequently, the affair is neither an amusement nor a casual fling, but rather a crisis that must be resolved in one direction or the other. For other personality types an extramarital sexual relationship may have less significant emotional effect.

One important aspect of the effects of extramarital sexual relationships involves the reaction of the spouse. Not surprisingly, the results of many studies show that the great majority of those involved in an affair report that their spouses reacted in a negative manner, including fear, rage, jealousy, humiliation, and depression. Some reacted by threatening divorce. Often, a divorce is the end result.

A person who discovers a mate's involvement in an affair and who does not express anger or hurt toward the spouse may instead focus negative feelings toward himself or herself. Turning anger and hurt inward may take the form of neglect of health or appearance, severe depression, suicide attempts, accidents, alcohol abuse, or other self-destructive behavior.

While an affair often results in divorce, the outcome of an extramarital affair rarely results in marriage to the extramarital partner. Researcher Morton Hunt found that only one in ten of those interviewed had married or intended to marry the person with whom they were having the affair. Even when the divorces are initiated in order to marry the extramarital partner, the intended marriages take place only about 50 percent of the time.

Marriage to the extramarital partner usually does not take place largely because the selection of an extramarital partner is often poor in terms of compatibility. Often the extramarital relationship is much less comfortable than is the relationship with the spouse.[3]

AFFAIR PROOFING YOUR MARRIAGE

Any couple can take certain steps which will greatly reduce the chances that their marriage will be impacted by an affair. Basically, affair proofing your marriage involves doing everything you can do to enrich your marriage. It includes spending time together and it certainly requires making your marriage relationship a top priority. There are specific strategies which have helped many successful couples to affair proof their marriages.

Consider the Consequences

Many people become involved in an affair with little or no thought about the probable consequences. Some unrealistically think an affair will have no negative effect on their marriage. Many actually believe no one else will ever know about the affair.

"I have been very attracted to two other women during the 35 years that Myra and I have been married," confessed Carl. "I worked with both of them but at different time periods. There was a strong physical attraction. But in both instances there was more: We could talk easily to each other and we had common interests.

"They were both attracted to me," confessed Carl. "I think an affair could have naturally developed in either or both cases."

Carl shared that the critical strategy that was most important in preventing him from slipping into these affairs was that he was able to look ahead and consider the probable consequences. "I thought about what would most likely happen if I started an affair," said Carl.

"I did not like the scenarios that marched before me. I knew it was unrealistic to think that people at work would not find out. I envisioned the gossip and what they would think of me for being unfaithful to my wife. I would definitely lose the respect of my co-workers and the working conditions would become more negative," said Carl. "Someone would tell Myra."

"Then, most of all, I saw the great hurt it would bring to Myra. Did I want to risk losing the great marriage relationship I enjoyed? Would I want her to leave and take the kids away? The answer was no. Too many problems and heartaches would come with having an affair. It was not worth it. I am thankful I had enough sense to realize that," said Carl.

Couples who are successful in affair proofing their marriage all have the ability to do what Carl did. They can look ahead and envision realistically what the probable consequences will be. And they judge that an affair isn't worth the price.

Avoid Placing Yourself in Vulnerable Situations

Many people who have affairs report a major reason they became involved is they were in a situation where the opportunity is present and the temptation is high. An important strategy for preventing affairs is simply to avoid placing ourselves in vulnerable situations.

"I found myself becoming interested in a teacher at the school where I teach," said Shannon. "I worked closely with him on a number of projects so there were numerous opportunities for us to get to know each other.

"We both attended a conference in California and it was there that I felt the greatest temptation. The opportunity was perfect. No one else from our town was there. No one would have known. He made an overture after an especially romantic lunch and I declined. But it was hard on me because the circumstances were so conducive to starting an affair."

Shannon made up her mind that she would never place herself in that kind of situation again. "I turned down opportunities to go to conferences that he was attending. I also avoided working alone with him. In time, I requested and was given a transfer to another school in town where I would not have to work with him at all. This change was a big help and after a few months my infatuation with him faded. It was critical for me to avoid putting myself in tempting situations."

Build Your Partner's Self-Esteem

One of the major reasons that people have affairs is to enhance their self-esteem and to feel desirable. They like the feeling of being courted. Having an affair may make them feel young again. Armed with this insight, one of the most important actions a couple can take to prevent an affair is to make a conscious effort to build each other's self-esteem. Spouses who cultivate the art of expressing genuine appreciation to each other hold a key to marriage happiness and to affair proofing their marriage.

When two people consistently give each other sincere compliments and build each other up psychologically, they create a positive atmosphere where they make each other feel good. Because they enhance each other's self-esteem they enjoy being together and are much less likely to be attracted to someone else in order to feel good about themselves.

Keep Romance in the Marriage

Couples who have successfully affair proofed their marriages have made a conscious effort to keep romance and a sense of adventure in their relationships. They court each other, write love notes, go out on dates with each other, send flowers, and have fun together. They surprise each other and do the unexpected sometimes. They create a sense of adventure and spontaneity in their marriage. Couples who keep romance and a sense of adventure in their marriage do not have to seek an experience with someone else that will make them feel romantic and young again.

Special Time Together

Intimacy is one of the deepest needs we have and it is one of the most strongly desired qualities we expect to receive from a marriage relationship. Experiencing the intimacy we desire from our marriage relationship requires an investment of time. We must spend large quantities of unhurried time together in a marriage relationship in order to create an atmosphere which is conducive to the development of intimacy.

It is ironic that couples desire intimacy and expect to find intimacy in their marriages. Yet, they lead life styles which make it impossible to find intimacy in their relationship. They never spend any relaxed time together where they can have real communication with each other. They lead frantic lifestyles and fragmented lives that are highly stressful. Both are preoccupied with careers and neglect their relationship. An emptiness grows in their lives and they may question if there is not more to life. They yearn for the intimacy that is missing in their lives and they may search for it in an extramarital affair.

One of the best ways to affair proof your marriage is to invest good measures of time in your marriage relationship. Successful couples spend a great deal of relaxed time together where they communicate; have fun; listen to each other's hopes, dreams, irritations, and joys. They enjoy sharing hobbies and common interests. They spend a lot of time simply "hanging out" together.

Time is the most precious gift you and your spouse can give to each other. Give it generously for it generates the intimacy you both desire and it does much to affair proof your marriage.

Chapter 8

WEATHERING THE STORMS OF LIFE

A ll marriages, no matter how strong or happy, will encounter tough times. That is because all married couples live in a real world where bad things happen and hard times come to all people. The happy couples in our Marriage Success Research Project had experienced the toughest of tough times. They had gone through crises such as a life-threatening illness; death of a loved one; unemployment; loss of a farm, ranch or family business that had been in the family for generations; and teenage children addicted to drugs. Yet these successful couples responded to these difficult times effectively. They survived the most severe crises and came out with a stronger marriage. Many of us also know of other marriages, however, that have not survived those same crises. What makes the difference? What enabled these happy couples to weather the storms of life?

COMMUNICATION AND MUTUAL SUPPORT

Two of the strategies that successful couples reported as being most helpful in dealing with crisis times are so interwoven that it is nearly impossible to separate them. These two strategies augment each other. Each one is made more effective by the practice of the other. These two strategies are communication with each other and mutual support.

"Just being able to talk with Wade has been so important to me in getting through the worst of our crises," said Dee. "Sharing our feelings with each other and just talking through the situation a number of times is therapeutic.

"We problem-solve together. No matter how bad the situation may be, it is a good feeling to know the two of us are a team working together to deal with it.

"We help each other. When I am down and really discouraged, Wade lifts me up. He gives me encouragement and hope when I need it most. When he is down I encourage him. It is good that we don't usually hit our low points at the same time."

Successful couples do not leave one partner to deal with a crisis or problem alone. They support each other and unite to deal with the problem together. This is a major reason why they are successful in dealing with tough times. They combine their expertise, thoughts and energies, and this joint approach to the problem gives the couple confidence that they can deal with it successfully.

LOOKING FOR THE RAINBOW

"When I was a child I was very afraid of thunderstorms," shared a Texas husband. "One day when I was visiting my grandmother we had a very severe storm. She tried to comfort me as the lightning flashed and the thunder boomed – without much success. Just as the storm was over she called me to come outside. 'There,' she said, pointing toward the sky, 'look at that beautiful rainbow.' I stood looking at the rainbow for a few minutes. Then grandmother told me that I should always look for the rainbow after the storm," he said. "After that I was never as afraid of storms.

"I have used this in dealing with the difficult times in my life. My wife and I look for rainbows in life's storms and it really helps. We are more effective in dealing with tough times because we can see the positives."

The happy couples in our Marriage Success Research Project have the ability to see something positive in a bad situation. Regardless of how dark the crisis or tragedy, they look for and find the silver linings in the clouds. They then focus on those positives.

Often the positives are simple things such as: "I am so thankful that you are by my side and we can face this thing together," or "You have a wonderful sense of humor and it is a boost for my mental health," or "This is a bad situation but we are fortunate to have a number of things in our lives to help us get through this crisis."

The ability to focus on something good in a bad situation helps a couple to keep a more balanced perspective and to avoid becoming so discouraged and despondent that they cannot function. Looking for and being able to see the silver linings in the dark clouds does something else, too. It gives the couple a sense of well-being even in the midst of the storm. It heightens their awareness of their resources and assets. Concentrating on the good in a bad situation increases confidence and optimism about dealing with the problem.[1]

GOT LEMONS? MAKE LEMONADE

Not only do couples with happy, lasting marriages look for the good in a bad situation, they also look for opportunities to produce something good out of a difficult situation. They overcome difficulties and sorrows by being active in making some good things happen. As the bumper sticker says, "When life gives you lemons – make lemonade!"

The ancient Chinese symbol for crisis is a combination of two symbols: the symbol for danger and the symbol for opportunity. A crisis of any kind can be a difficult time in a marriage. It is an unstable, stressful time. But a crisis is also an opportunity if it is viewed positively and creatively. It can be a catalyst for growth of the marriage and the individual. It can be the beginning of better times.

Amanda and Fred faced the kind of crisis that has devastated many individuals and destroyed many marriages. One dreadful morning (at 2 a.m.), they received a call from the police informing them that their daughter had been murdered. She had been shot during a robbery at the convenience store where she worked; she was only 21 years old at the time. They alternated between numbing shock and unbearable pain.

"I felt like I was in a dream – a nightmare. It all seemed unreal," recalled Amanda. "There were times when I didn't think I could go on. I kept waiting to wake up from this nightmare – but of course I couldn't. For the first few months it was a challenge just to get through each day. I had to keep my mind occupied with something besides the loss of our daughter. I just couldn't think about it a lot. This may sound silly but I couldn't face making it through a whole day. So I would think, 'I can make it through ten minutes.' And so I would break down the day into little compartments. For example, I would count the number of steps it took to go from our front door to where our car was parked in the garage. Then I would count the number of steps it took to go from where I parked the car at work to my office."

Amanda mentioned something else that motivated her and Fred not to allow themselves to be destroyed by this ordeal. "Fred reminded me often of his love and that we still had two younger children who depended on us," said Amanda. "I would also remind him of our children's needs when he was feeling especially depressed. This reminded us that our lives had a purpose and real meaning to someone besides the two of us."

Fred added that thinking of the two younger children helped them both to remember that they had much for which to be thankful. "We had the blessings of our two youngest children," said Fred. "Thankfully we had not lost them and they needed us. I think this helped us to begin to search for other good things in this tragedy.

"The way you look at what has happened to you makes all the difference in how you deal with it," noted Fred. "For example, some other good things we focused on were that we did not have to go for months or years not knowing what had happened to our daughter – as might have been the case if she had been kidnapped. We were thankful that we had each other. We were blessed with good friends and a loving support network at our church. Both Amanda and I were fortunate to have helpful, compassionate bosses and co-workers.

"There are other examples we could mention," said Fred. "But thinking about these good things in our lives helped us to feel more capable of overcoming our terrible loss."

Amanda shared one other creative action which she and Fred took that has been an immense help to their family. They purposely created beauty out of tragedy.

"We wanted to do something to turn the ugliness and sorrow into an experience of beauty and good that could be shared by others," said Amanda. "We designed a large, beautiful garden area at our church in memory of our daughter. We planted flowers and shrubs so that something is blooming or has colorful leaves or berries all year long. We included benches so that people could sit and meditate or pray. Many people have found comfort and peace there. Our daughter – who loved flowers – would be pleased."

SPIRITUAL FAITH

When we are hit by a crisis we usually feel overwhelmed. We may feel as if we are in a house in the middle of a hurricane with waves and wind pounding away – shaking it off its very foundation.

Drawing upon spiritual resources during such times helps many couples to overcome adversities that they did not think they could handle alone. When we asked the couples in our Marriage Success Research Project what had been most helpful to them in dealing with the most severe crisis of their marriage, the most often reported answers were prayer and spiritual faith.

"I was sitting alone in our study and the only thoughts going through my mind were of suicide," said Shaun. "The ranch had been in my family for four generations. And now I had lost it.

"Things had been going downhill for the last few years and we just couldn't keep it up any more," Shaun continued. "We had to declare bankruptcy and lost the ranch. Even though it was not all my fault, I felt like I had let down my father, my grandfather, and my great grandfather. I felt like a total failure. All their work for so many years was just gone."

Shaun desperately needed some relief from his pain and a change in the direction his life had taken. Somehow he knew suicide was not the answer – even though he didn't know what the answer was.

"I fell to my knees and I prayed aloud, ' God, please help me and guide me. I can't do this by myself.' Over and over I kept repeating that. While I was still on my knees, my wife, Bonita, came in and knelt beside me. We prayed together. We asked God to help us to place ourselves in His hands and trust Him. We asked God to give us guidance and peace about the situation.

"After this time in prayer together I felt a strange sense of peace. It was strange in that moments before the prayer I had been tormented by thoughts of suicide."

A few days later doubts began to plague Shaun again. " I had come to peace and acceptance about losing the ranch but I worried about our future. I had no idea what kind of a job I would get or where we would live.

"I expressed these concerns to Bonita. Her reply to me was, 'Shaun, didn't we place this in God's hands and ask Him to guide us? God will certainly guide us. We need to be patient and let His plan unfold.' "

She read a passage to Shaun from Psalm 46:1-2: "God is our refuge and strength, a very present help in trouble. Therefore, we will not fear, though the earth be removed, and though the mountains be caarried into the midst of the sea…"

"That passage had a profound impact upon me," said Shaun. "I memorized it and repeated it every day – especially when I felt fearful. I began to visualize God walking with me every day and helping me overcome this problem. My faith became deeper than it had ever been. This was a new level for me. My wife has always possessed deep spiritual faith which was a great blessing to me in getting through this crisis."

Shaun and Bonita did successfully overcome this crisis. They moved to town and Shaun began a career in tractor sales – something he enjoyed and did very well. Bonita found a position as a teacher's aide at the elementary school – something she had wanted to do for some time but could not because they had lived so far out of town.

COMMITMENT

A prominent quality emerged among the successful couples with lasting marriages that provides a clear insight into why they deal with crises successfully. They have a deep commitment to love and support each other in good times and bad times. Their commitment to each other generates another commitment to overcome whatever crisis or tough time that may come their way. In a sense, the decision is already made in their minds that they will prevail and not allow tough times to destroy their relationship.

Vivian and Al enjoyed a good, strong marriage that – like all marriages – was not perfect. One of those imperfections grew into a problem that shook their marriage relationship and their lives like an earthquake. They had been married almost 27 years when they were faced with a crisis that would have destroyed most marriages.

Al was a very well-known local politician – the mayor of his home town. A friendly, personable man, Al was also an effective and well-esteemed mayor. He had a genuine concern for the people in his community. He and Vivian had led successful fund raising drives for various charities. Because of Al's career success and celebrity status he and Vivian had enjoyed a high income for several years. They had a beautiful home and all the material possessions they wanted. They were actively involved in their church. Their life seemed perfect.

Everyone was shocked when the front page of the newspaper and the evening news on television revealed a lawsuit was being filed against Al by a woman he had worked with for several years. The charge was sexual harassment

At first, Vivian did not believe the charges. She trusted Al completely; he was gentle and kind. He loved her and their children. She defended him fiercely. It had to be a mistake.

Soon, however, Vivian had to face the disturbing truth that there was substance to the charge. As the lawsuit proved to have some basis, Vivian had to deal with a bitter disappointment in Al.

As the drama unfolded, it came to light that Al had carried on a six-year affair with the woman. Al admitted the affair but contended that it had begun by mutual agreement. He had not pressured her to begin a relationship. He was, however, her supervisor. Shortly before the lawsuit was filed he had reassigned her to another position so that they would not be working so closely together. Al was trying to end their affair. She considered the reassignment a demotion. They had quarreled – loudly and in public. And then she found a lawyer.

Vivian was embarrassed and ashamed, as was Al. She felt betrayed. Not only did Al betray her trust but he had carried on the affair for six years and she had not been aware of it. She felt stupid and terribly naïve. Pain and discomfort were inflicted on Vivian anew everyday by the media. Their coverage of this local gossipy news was continuous.

After months of intense scrutiny and upheaval of their lives the lawsuit was eventually settled out of court. The woman was awarded a substantial amount of money from Al's business. Al was asked to resign as mayor.

Now the crisis expanded from the affair to serious financial loss. In addition, Vivian was advised and pressured by some of her friends that she should divorce Al.

Consider the stress and strain on this marriage: the pain and threat of a long-term affair, the embarrassment and disgrace of such a lawsuit, the constant barrage by the media, forced resignation of Al as mayor, and the substantial financial loss. Uncertainty now existed in just about every aspect of their lives.

What are the odds that this marriage would last? If you said slim to none, most marriage counselors would agree with your assessment. But Vivian and Al beat the odds.

Vivian's commitment to Al and their marriage remained strong. Instead of blaming him, or taking revenge, she turned her efforts to supporting and encouraging Al. She did everything she could to repair his badly damaged self-esteem. Her actions communicated an important message to Al. She was standing by him. And through all the ugly mess she loved him and would always love him.

"I had to get through a lot of bad feelings," Vivian recalled. "I cried a lot and went through some rough periods of depression and anger. I was ashamed. I was scared. Sometimes, I did think about divorce. What helped me the most was prayer. I asked God to help me to truly forgive Al and to let go of the destructive emotions I was holding inside.

"This did not happen quickly," said Vivian. "But gradually I felt a complete release from the depression and anger. I finally was able to really let it go and I knew we were beginning a new and better chapter of our lives."

Al made the decision to renew his commitment to their marriage. "Words could never describe how much Vivian's commitment and support meant to me," Al said. "I am sorry that I put her through that kind of hurt.

"If there is any good thing that came out of this mess it is that I was reminded of the many good things in our marriage and that I am lucky to have a partner like Vivian.

"I did a lot of thinking about the way I had been living from day to day," Al continued, "I had become so caught up in my career that I was neglecting my marriage. I was spending all of my time in my work. It happened gradually and I had become more and more materialistic in terms of what drove me. I had become puffed up with my self-importance which is what led to the affair.

"I decided to get back to the values I had formerly lived by. I made the commitment that Vivian and our marriage would come first in my heart. They would no longer take a back seat to my job."

Both Al and Vivian report that their marriage is happier and stronger now than it has ever been. When Vivian was asked why she had not divorced Al, she replied, "You don't just throw away 27 years of a marriage – 27 good years!"

Vivian continued with a statement which gives insight into her value system and which is powerful in its ramifications: "In a very real way, I had already made that decision years ago when I made my wedding vows to Al. I promised to stay by him in good times and in bad times."

Vivian and Al faced many changes in their lives. Al found a new job and they moved to a different part of the country. Their income was less and they had to adjust to a lower standard of living. They rose above these challenges and weathered a severe storm in their marriage because they drew strength from a strong commitment – a commitment that was decided long before the crisis came.

CULTIVATING A SUPPORT NETWORK

A happy couple with a lasting marriage will look to each other most of all for support during a crisis. But they also cultivate a good support network among friends, their extended family, church, and professional social service resources. They know where to go for help.

Amanda and Fred utilized their support network to help them to get through the tragic loss of their daughter. "We had friends who were a great comfort to us at that time," said Amanda. "People from our church were such a help. They brought food, made some telephone calls that had to be made. They cleaned house. I don't know what we would have done without them."

"I think the most important thing about the support we received is that it let us know there are people who care about us," added Fred.

Amanda responded to the question of what happened after most of the friends and extended family had stopped coming to see them after a few weeks had passed. "Of course this is a natural thing to happen," she said. "People have to get back to their normal, daily lives.

"There were very rough moments we experienced for a long time after the immediate support had left," she said. "My sister has always been a very optimistic, encouraging person. She and her husband were the two people who were the greatest help to us.

"So when we were in our lowest valleys we would call them and say 'We really need you to be here with us for a few days,' " Amanda said. "They would always come. It meant so much to us."

Fred also indicated that, "At one point we received professional counseling. We did not do that long but it was helpful during the time we did it."

Amanda and Fred demonstrate how important support networks are to couples with successful, lasting marriages in overcoming crises. They have good support from their friends, relatives, church and others in the community. They know where to go for professional help and seek professional counseling when they feel they need it.

It is important that Amanda and Fred did not just wait for the support to come. When the support was not immediately available and they felt a deep need for it, they took the initiative in seeking that support.

SETTING SPECIFIC GOALS

A strategy which many happy couples report helps them to get through a crisis is to set specific goals and then work together to meet those goals. Sometimes the goals may be routine and not appear to be directly related to the crisis but yet can be very helpful in getting through it. Remember the example of Amanda setting herself the goal of getting from day to day and activity to activity? She broke things down into small compartments. She identified one goal as just getting from her front door to the car. She counted the number of steps it took. This enabled her to think about something other than the terrible loss she had experienced. She also experienced some satisfaction and feeling of progress by successfully completing this short-term goal.

Audra and Wayne, like many couples, had experienced serious financial trouble. Setting specific goals is one important way they overcame it.

"We were at the point of bankruptcy," said Wayne. "We almost took that option, but we decided if there were any other way to get through the financial quicksand we would take it. Fortunately other possibilities did work out.

"We consolidated our debts and took several other actions that helped," he explained. "It was a big problem and felt overwhelming. It was easy to be discouraged because it seemed like we could never get out from under all that debt.

"I think one of the most helpful steps for us was to establish specific goals that we could realistically accomplish and then to work toward meeting those goals," said Wayne.

"One goal we set was to stop writing so many checks," he continued. "We had been writing checks for everything and it was hard to ever know how much money we really had. Sometimes we'd forget to record a check or two – or to calculate our balance. As a result we were continually overdrawing. And paying big bank charges for overdrafts.

"We worked together to accomplish this goal by writing only six checks a month. One was for the mortgage payment, the second was for the car payment, the third was for our insurance, and the others were for utilities.

"Everything else we paid with cash," explained Wayne. "Each month we put cash in envelopes for each expense. For example, we had an envelope for groceries, an envelope for gas, and one for entertainment. We knew the amount of money in each envelope was all we could spend for that expense for the month. With this approach we always knew how much money we had left.

"It helped us to manage our expenditures a lot better," said Wayne. "We certainly accomplished our goal of writing fewer checks and we felt good about that."

But money wasn't their only trouble. Wayne and Audra had both become more irritable, depressed and hostile as their financial stress had grown more serious. They had grown more irritable with each other but also with their children.

"Wayne and I talked about how we had allowed ourselves to

become more negative," shared Audra. "We did not like that. It was affecting the children, our marriage, and everyone we came in contact with in a bad way. We had lost any joy in living."

"We decided we did not have to behave this way," said Audra. "So we set for ourselves a specific way of being more positive and kind to each other. We worked toward the goal of becoming more fun to be around. After all, being pleasant and a little more cheerful wouldn't make us have any less money. We consciously reduced our hostile, pessimistic talk and responses in half by the end of two weeks. We spent some family time doing fun (and inexpensive) things together. We counted our blessings.

"We were successful," she said. "And it made a big difference in how we all felt. We certainly enjoyed each other more and this more positive attitude helped us to more effectively deal with our financial problems."

Chapter 9

DEVELOPING A GREAT SEXUAL RELATIONSHIP

Psychotherapist, Erich Fromm, maintained that sexual desire reflects the human need for love and union. The need for intimacy is interwoven throughout sexual relationships and is more powerful than the purely physical aspects of sex. It is true that a sexual relationship may exist without intimacy. But rarely will a sexual relationship be completely fulfilling without intimacy.

The reason why intimacy is so closely linked to a satisfying sexual relationship may be found in the definition of sexuality. To some persons sex is only physical and is separate from other parts of their lives. Pornography is an example of this extreme view and portrays a pattern of exploitation of people as sex objects. When sex is viewed and practiced in this manner, intimacy is lost and relationships are empty and shallow. Because people are not seen as whole persons, it is easier to exploit them and ignore emotions.

Sexuality involves everything about us that makes us male or female. It obviously includes the physical. But sexuality is more than that. Our sexuality also includes our emotions, our social relationships, our values, ethics, morals, and spiritual faith. It also involves our intellect and our decision-making and problem-solving skills. Our good judgment (or bad judgment) is certainly reflected in our sexual behavior.

Our sexuality is connected to every other part of our lives. For this reason an understanding of sexuality requires that it be viewed in a wholistic manner – within the context of the total person and the total relationship.

HAZARDS TO SEXUAL RELATIONSHIPS

A number of common hazards can cause a couple problems in their sexual relationship. As we examine some of the major factors which prevent couples from experiencing satisfaction in their sexual relationship, we can gain insights into improving sexual relationships.

A NEGATIVE, NON-SUPPORTIVE INTERPERSONAL RELATIONSHIP

Ben and Dot live in constant conflict. They hurl insults and put-downs at each other. Ben is very sarcastic and often ridicules Dot in public. Dot is less direct in lashing out at Ben but makes snide remarks and veiled criticisms.

Mildred and Albert spend very little time together. They are too busy to have any real conversations or to show much interest in each other's lives. Mildred suspects Albert may be having an affair and is lying to her about it.

The sexual relationships of both of these couples are bleak. This is not surprising since their total marriage relationships are not happy.

These two couples demonstrate an important principle: The sexual relationship and the total interpersonal relationship are closely intertwined. Some people believe that a good sexual relationship will make the rest of the relationship good and if the sexual relationship goes down hill then so does the rest of the relationship. According to clinical and research evidence, this belief is a myth because the emphasis is backwards. The truth of the matter is that the quality of the total relationship is far more likely to influence the quality of the sexual relationship than vice versa.

A negative, non-supportive interpersonal relationship between a couple can do more to harm the sexual relationship than almost anything else. When a husband and wife develop a threatening pattern of interaction in which they criticize, complain, blame, put each other down and hurt each other's self esteem, they minimize their chances of experiencing sexual happiness with each other.

BOREDOM

Simple boredom with the daily routine of life and/or the marriage relationship can be a major barrier to a satisfying sexual relationship. Couples can become indifferent to each other largely because of preoccupation with work, children, hobbies or other areas of their lives. In turn they allow their sexual relationship to become so monotonous that they actually replace sexual activities with work, television, or other leisure time activities.

ANXIETY AND DEPRESSION

Brad and Leanne have been married for six years. During the last three months, the frequency of their sexual encounters has sharply decreased. Brad has felt little desire for sexual intimacy because he has been experiencing some difficulty in maintaining an erection.

Leanne was puzzled. Why had this change occurred? They had a good, solid marriage. Fortunately they could talk to each other even though Brad was embarrassed initially. As they talked, they began to understand the problem.

Leanne came to realize that Brad was under tremendous stress at work. He had a new boss who was hostile and controlling. Rumors were flying that the company was going to downsize and Brad felt his job was in jeopardy.

Anxiety and depression are detrimental to both sexual desire and the ability to function sexually. Outside sources of stress such as work conflict, loss of job, or concerns about health can cause a person to become preoccupied to the extent of not being able to concentrate upon the sexual relationship. Husbands and wives who find their sexual relationship suddenly decreasing in satisfaction often discover that one or both partners are worried, anxious, or depressed about something. An understanding spouse, such as Leanne, who can help the other partner come to terms with his or her anxiety or depression often can help the partner to deal effectively with the source of stress and at the same time help to restore their sexual relationship.

FATIGUE

Latesha and Kirk work all day at demanding jobs. After work they pick up their two preschoolers from daycare, stop for some groceries, and make a second stop to get the clothes at the dry cleaners. When they arrive home they cook dinner, feed two dogs and a cat, run a load of laundry, vacuum the floors, wash dishes, read to their children and get them ready for bed. By the time all these things are done, Latesha and Kirk are exhausted. All they want to do is watch a little television for relaxation. When they finish watching the late news they are so sleepy that they don't have the energy to talk and certainly don't feel like having a sexual encounter. They stumble into bed and fall asleep.

Like stress, fatigue also interferes with sexual desire and with sexual responsiveness. Couples can minimize the problem by purposely planning for sexual interactions at a time of the day when they are less likely to be fatigued.

PHYSICAL PROBLEMS

Jake and Malinda began having sexual problems after ten years of marriage. The nature of the problem was that they suddenly seemed incompatible sexually because Malinda desired to have sex more frequently than did Jake.

"It bothered me a lot," said Malinda. "I worried about what had caused the change. Did he not find me attractive anymore? Was I doing something to turn him off sexually? I even began to suspect that he might be having an affair."

Malinda would kiss Jake or cuddle up with him. However, Jake usually was not very responsive. "He would tell me he was coming to bed soon but he would delay until I had fallen asleep. He would stay up late on the computer or watching television," said Malinda. "I felt like he just did not want to be with me."

In reality, this was far from the truth as far as Jake was concerned. Over the past several months Jake had experienced a few instances in which he had not been able to achieve an erection at all, which mortified him. Because of those experiences he was fearful of putting himself in that situation again with Malinda. He did not want to fail again so he simply avoided the possibility.

Malinda persisted until Jake agreed to see a marriage counselor. The counselor immediately asked if Jake had seen a physician. When Jake said that he had not, the marriage counselor suggested that he see a physician very soon.

A complete and thorough physical exam revealed that Jake had diabetes. He hadn't realized that he had diabetes or that it could be the reason for his erectile difficulties. Upon knowing this, medical steps were taken to help Jake successfully achieve erection and to manage his diabetes.

Anything which undermines our health can negatively affect our sexual functioning. Some physical illnesses and diseases, such as diabetes, interfere significantly with sexual functioning.

Certain physical changes caused by aging may make sexual intercourse painful in older women. The vaginal walls of older women tend to become thinner and less flexible; also, less lubricating secretions are produced. These changes often result in sexual intercourse being painful. However, it is encouraging that such problems can be remedied rather easily medically and through the use of sterile, water-soluble lubricants.

Men, as they age, experience a reduction in the male hormone, testosterone which is responsible for the sex drive. Testosterone levels in men between the ages of 50 and 70 decrease to less than one-half of that produced between the ages of 23 and 36. Because of the natural reduction in testosterone level over the years, many men experience a substantial decrease in sexual drive and responsiveness. They are also more likely to experience erectile problems because of the decreasing testosterone level.[1] Fortunately, this condition can be helped medically by testosterone replacement therapy.

The most common sexual problem among aging men is prostate gland trouble. Prostate problems, which can cause impotence, plague about 10 percent of the male population at age 40 and about 50 percent of those at age 80. Fortunately, when prostate problems are treated early, the chances for maintaining satisfying sexual relationships are excellent.

PREOCCUPATION WITH PERFORMANCE

In our culture, much importance is placed on being "sexy" and sexually adept. As a result some people become very concerned with their performance. For example, many women's difficulty in reaching orgasm is directly related to their excessive worry about whether they will have an orgasm or not.

Lillian had read some misleading popular magazine articles which suggested that most women experience multiple orgasms. The message Lillian got from these articles was that she should have multiple orgasms and that there was something wrong with her sexual responsiveness or with her sexual partner if she didn't.

She became very determined to have multiple orgasms and so tense about it that she was often not able to experience an orgasm at all. Because of this preoccupation, her sexual relationship with her husband had, in her own mind, moved from a context of pleasure to a context of performance.

Lillian felt inadequate, disappointed, and resentful. She worried about what was causing her orgasmic dysfunction. She and her husband eventually went to a sex therapist. The problem soon began to improve when Lillian learned from the therapist that fewer than 15 percent of all women actually experience multiple orgasms. The therapist encouraged Lillian to stop being concerned about achieving orgasm and to just simply enjoy the pleasure of the sexual relationship with her husband. With assistance from the therapist, Lillian was soon able to stop being concerned with performance and once again experienced happiness and satisfaction in her sexual relationship.

Men are particularly vulnerable to being preoccupied with sexual performance. This is because they define themselves more narrowly than do women. Many men see their worth as men as being determined by their job performance, the money they earn, and their sexual prowess. Frequently, the result is that these men, like Lillian, shift their emphasis from giving and receiving pleasure with their partner to a context of performance. They approach their sexual interaction in much the same way they do a job evaluation or a golf tournament. This approach often generates anxiety and tension and may contribute to impotency problems.

SUBSTANCE ABUSE

The abuse of substances such as marijuana or alcohol can interfere with sexual functioning. Alcohol is one of the most famous of alleged aphrodisiacs. In reality it does not serve as a sexual stimulant. In some individuals, the moderate consumption of alcohol may temporarily remove certain inhibitions, fear, and guilt concerning sexual behavior.

In truth, alcohol is a depressant. When taken in considerable quantity, alcohol deadens the nerves, narcotizes the brain, retards reflexes, dilates blood vessels, and interferes with the ability to achieve an erection. Shakespeare summed it up in *Macbeth,* "It [alcohol] provokes the desire, but it takes away the performance."

Some maintain that the use of marijuana heightens sexual pleasures. However, marijuana is not an aphrodisiac. There is evidence that the continual, substantial use of marijuana actually lowers the testosterone level and leads to decreased sexual desire and behavior.[2] For some individuals the physical expression of sex takes more initiative than they feel like expending; use of marijuana makes them sleepy and letharagic.

Addiction to most drugs, including alcohol, leads to a decrease in sexual desire and eventually to sexual impotence. For example, research indicates that approximately 95 percent of heroin addicts are sexually impotent.

The major way drugs such as heroin and cocaine work is to activate the sensual or pleasure centers in the body. These pleasure centers are primarily sexual in nature. Stimulation of the pleasure centers by drugs can soon replace normal sexual experiences as well as other forms of pleasures, such as eating. Most drug addicts have very little sex life because they have cultivated other types of sensual stimulation.

FACTORS THAT PROMOTE A GOOD SEXUAL RELATIONSHIP

The success of a sexual relationship is not just a matter of physiological factors. Because it is integrated with the total relationship, the satisfaction of the sexual relationship is strongly influenced by various aspects of the total marriage relationship. Couples who have a happy marriage typically have a satisfying sexual relationship. There are reasons. The following are among the most important influences contributing to a satisfying sexual relationship.

A TOTAL RELATIONSHIP THAT IS LOVING AND SUPPORTIVE

Nothing is more important to help a couple experience a satisfying sexual relationship than a positive, loving interpersonal environment characterized by genuine, mutual care and concern. A relationship of mutual respect, understanding, and being responsive to each other's needs creates a climate that is conducive to sexual responsiveness.

"Eric is honest", said Lindsey. "I never have to worry about whether he is telling the truth or wonder what he really means by a comment. He is upfront and I like that. I know I can trust him and I think that has helped our sex life.

"One thing Eric often does that is a real turn on for me is that he will leave little love notes. Sometimes he brings me flowers with a note that says 'Beautiful flowers for a beautiful lady'. These things make me feel special," she emphasized. "It's nice to feel like your husband admires you."

BEING PSYCHOLOGICALLY COMFORTABLE WITH EACH OTHER

Jeremy and Pat have a strained relationship which is adversely affecting their sex life. Pat is very competitive and dominant. She often uses mind games designed to make Jeremy lose his self-confidence. Jeremy has come to feel increasingly uncomfortable around Pat. He has lost interest in being with her and avoids having sex with her.

Comfort is an important but largely ignored quality of successful interpersonal relationships. Surprisingly, many husbands and wives do not feel comfortable with each other. Being uncomfortable with a partner can make it difficult to respond sexually. Two basic reasons for a lack of comfort in a relationship are distrust and a feeling that commitment is lacking. A couple can increase their psychological comfort together by being emotionally supportive of each other through mutual respect and care. Another way to create psychological comfort is by minimizing threatening behavior such as criticism and ridicule.

COMMITMENT

The presence of commitment is a major characteristic of happily married couples who have a satisfying sexual relationship. The world-renowned sex researchers, William Masters and Virginia Johnson, on the basis of their research and clinical experience conclude that commitment is the single most important factor contributing to satisfaction in a sexual relationship.[3] For example, it is interesting that some research indicates that women who have difficulty in experiencing orgasm tend to feel there is a lack of commitment from others close to them.

Both men and women tend to be more sexually responsive when they know their partner has a high degree of commitment toward them. Commitment encourages trust and psychological comfort which in turn generates security that allows spouses to give themselves freely in a sexual relationship. The freedom and safety to give oneself completely and spontaneously to a spouse enhances the intensity of the sexual relationship. Happily married couples have discovered that they become better lovers as they become more committed .

CULTIVATING A RELAXED ATTITUDE OF ENJOYMENT

A powerful influence in experiencing a happy, satisfying sexual relationship is for spouses to cultivate a relaxed attitude and approach to their sexual interaction. A couple increases their happiness and satisfaction as they concentrate on simply enjoying the sexual experience and the pleasure they bring to each other.

Couples who have a high degree of satisfaction in their sexual relationship do not place much emphasis on performance. They do not think or worry about how they are measuring up or whether or not they have orgasms, how intense the orgasms are, or how many. To do so creates tension and anxiety and tends to remove sexual interaction from its pleasurable context.

GOOD COMMUNICATION

Happy couples with a high degree of satisfaction in their sexual relationship tend to have good communication patterns. Communication can help a couple avoid many problems and promote a high degree of satisfaction. When a husband and wife can communicate the types of sexual behavior that please and displease them, they increase their probability of experiencing a good sexual relationship.

When a couple spend a lot of time talking with each other and communicating positive messages such as appreciation, their total relationship is strengthened. When they feel they can talk with each other about anything, their psychological comfort is enhanced and they feel closer to each other. This in turn creates a climate which promotes a positive sexual relationship.

KNOWING THE SEXUAL RESPONSE CYCLE

Possessing basic knowledge of the physiological aspects of the sexual response cycle can be very helpful in contributing to a more satisfying sexual relationship. Many couples, young and old, experience difficulties and frustrations in their sexual relationship simply because they are unaware of some of the differences in the sexual response cycle of men and women. Such difficulties can usually be quite easily resolved.

The body's physiological response to sexual stimulation is remarkably similar in all people. The extensive research of sex researchers, William Masters and Virginia Johnson, led to the conclusion that although individuals show variations in how they respond, the sexual response cycle has four phases.[4] Some important gender differences were identified.

Excitement Phase

This first phase may begin with any one of a variety of sexual stimuli. Music, candlelight, daydreams, or a kiss may initiate sexual arousal. The excitement phase is characterized by increased blood pressure, increased heart rate and the muscles becoming more tense. There is congestion of the genital blood vessels. Vaginal lubrication appears in the female and the male achieves an erection. An important difference between men and women at this stage is that men become excited much more quickly than do women. A man may pass through the excitement phase and proceed to the next stages before a woman becomes excited at all.

Plateau Phase

During the plateau phase the responses begun in the excitement phase, such as the increased heart rate and the congestion of the genital blood vessels, intensify. The plateau phase can vary considerably in duration. Some couples prolong this stage by decreasing stimulation.

Orgasm Phase

As sexual excitement reaches a peak the sexual tensions built up during the first two phases are released in an orgasm. The orgasm response involves contractions of the pelvic muscles and tightening of muscles in the face, feet, and hands for both men and women. Women experience involuntary vaginal contractions. The man's ejaculation releases about 500 million sperm.

Sometimes an orgasm is very intense and at other times may be mild. Fictional descriptions of orgasm usually depict it as a frenzied, wild emotional onslaught. But as with every other sexual response, each individual has a unique and personal reaction.

Differences in the sexual responses of men and women are apparent during this phase and may be the source of some dissatisfaction. Many men can reach orgasm within just a few minutes of sexual intercourse. In fact, Kinsey's landmark study of sexual behavior found that men typically reach orgasm within two minutes after sexual intercourse has been initiated. This is too quick for most women to achieve orgasm, or even to become excited, unless there has been sufficient foreplay.

Most women, however, can experience an orgasm within 15 minutes of foreplay and intercourse. For many men this will require careful monitoring of their behavior and of how quickly they proceed through the excitement and plateau phases.

Resolution phase

Following orgasm the body returns to its normal state. For example, blood pressure and pulse rate return to normal. This is called the resolution phase. There are important differences between men and women during this phase, too. Following orgasm, men experience a refractory period during which rearousal is impossible. Further stimulation of the penis is painful during this period. Because of this many men prefer an abrupt end to erotic play following orgasm, which may be frustrating to their spouses.

Women do not go through this same type of refractory period and consequently are not as likely to desire an abrupt end to erotic play following orgasm. The resolution phase is generally longer for women. Couples can experience a more satisfying sexual relationship by being aware of these differences and focusing on providing pleasure for each other.

THE SECRET IS...

Happily married couples who have a good sexual relationship share a profound message with us. The secret of sexual relationships that are highly satisfying is simple. The secret is not technique or overpowering good looks. The secret is developing a good total interpersonal relationship. Spouses who express genuine appreciation and admiration to each other, who are mutually considerate and affectionate, and who share a high degree of commitment and love create an interpersonal atmosphere that is conducive to the highest degree of sexual responsiveness.

Chapter 10

NURTURING SPIRITUAL WELLNESS

I n all of our research with successful, happy marriages no quality emerged as more important to marriage success than spiritual wellness. Time after time couples told us this was one of the most important reasons for their marriage success. Eight powerful qualities of spiritual wellness emerged among the successful couples. Each quality contributes to spiritual wellness. Together, these eight qualities create an effect on the marriage relationship that is greater than the sum of the parts.

A SPIRITUAL FAITH

The successful couples we researched gained strength, support, and serenity by drawing from a spiritual reservoir. Their ability to draw upon a spiritual resource flows from two sources.

First, they believe that God is a presence in their daily lives. And second, they trust in God to help them.

"We have learned to turn over our problems and needs to God and then depend on God to guide us," shared a midwestern wife. "Living this way has given us both much more optimism. We don't worry about things like we used to."

The successful couples report that the awareness of God in their day-to-day lives helps them to be more positive and supportive of each other. It helps them to be more understanding and less inclined to engage in hurtful actions.

"We pray and read the Bible daily," shares one husband. "It has made a huge difference in our marriage. I know that it has helped us to be less petty and less self-centered.

"I used to get angry very easily and stay mad a long time," he continued. "As I have grown in my spiritual faith, I don't get angry very often and I get over the anger more quickly. I don't criticize nearly as much either. These changes have made my wife's life a lot happier and have made our home more pleasant."

A sense of purpose is a dimension of their spiritual faith that strengthens the marriage relationship for these successful couples. Few things are as powerful as a focused sense of purpose.

"We feel that God has a purpose for us as a couple," said one Nebraska woman. "It makes us feel closer to each other knowing that we share this common purpose. It also gives our relationship a larger meaning and moves it beyond our basic wants and needs."

Couples who share a common purpose experience a strong bond that can give their life together a direction. Because they share a larger vision for their life together, it can help them rise above the stress, problems, and disappointments of life.

One such couple is Bob and Vernita. Their spiritual faith has led them to adopt children with disabilities. The powerful, driving purpose Bob and Vernita share is to provide a loving home for children that others would not adopt. They are wonderful, loving parents and their children are prospering.

Their lives are not easy. Bob and Vernita both have physical challenges themselves. Financial strain frequently has been severe and they have encountered many problems and setbacks.

Yet, this remarkable couple does not become obsessed with problems nor do they allow their setbacks to overwhelm them. They express great optimism and hope; their home is a happy place. Their 31-year marriage is strong and solid.

What makes the difference? Without hesitation, Bob and Vernita answer that their spiritual faith is the key. Also, when problems, stresses, or disappointments have come, Bob and Vernita have kept their focus on their powerful common purpose – to provide a loving, nurturing home for children who desperately need them. That common vision – an outgrowth of their spiritual faith – has given them a larger perspective and has helped them to deal successfully with their problems.

BE STILL

Cal and his wife, Evelyn, have been happily married for 40 years. They have successfully operated a farm with hundreds of acres of peach orchards. As all farmers do, Cal and Evelyn have experienced ups and down, disappointments, and many anxious moments worrying about whether there will be enough rain or if a late-spring freeze will kill the peach crop.

We asked Cal and Evelyn what they considered the most important reason for their marriage happiness in the midst of the stress and uncertainty of their farm life.

"Our spiritual faith," Cal said immediately. Evelyn agreed, adding, "It has helped us both to be patient, kind, and helpful to each other. It has helped us to not get stuck in the problem."

Cal indicated that not getting stuck in problems is a critical key. "If you allow that to happen," he said, "You become more irritable. You talk less. You begin to blame each other. You can become so tied up with the problems that you don't see each other or any hope."

Evelyn added, "We learned early in our marriage to pray for God's blessings and guidance, do the best we can, leave it in God's hands, and not worry about it. If we didn't have that faith and trust I think we would have gone crazy because so much of the yearly peach crop success is beyond our control."

We asked Cal and Evelyn how they had developed this deep spiritual faith and atmosphere in their marriage.

After thinking a moment, Cal answered, "By slowing down enough to see what is all around us."

Evelyn continued, "When we stop our head-long rush and frantic pace. When we stop our endless busyness and slow down. When we're still and quiet. Then we can see the beauty of God all around us and in each other more clearly."

Cal added "There are other things we have done to develop the spiritual atmosphere in our home like prayer, daily devotionals, going to church, and helping others. But for us a basic foundation is first to be still and know God is our God. We cannot do everything; the world does not rest on our shoulders."

"Being still is an art – a discipline," said Evelyn. "We deliberately take the time to see God's beauty in nature. We often walk through our orchard and marvel at the beauty – all these pink blossoms in spring and fragrant peaches in the summer. We take time everyday to see the good qualities in each other. We take time to be thankful. This has been important to our marriage and our mental and spiritual health."

Evelyn and Cal have discovered something vital for all the rest of us to know. Why? Because we live in such a busy, hurried world Our culture emphasizes materialism and uses technology to do things faster and faster. Each of us feels a great amount of emotional and physical stress just from the sheer volume of things to do each day. This type of cultural environment can easily crowd out spiritual thinking and meditation just as it can leave people with no time for relationships.

Evelyn and Cal, as well as many other successful couples we interviewed, have cultivated the "art of being still" as Evelyn described it. They have found that this practice enriches their spiritual wellness and the quality of their marriage relationship.

LOVE

Few words have been discussed more than love. Down through the centuries it has been a popular topic of poets and novelists. Yet, it is one of the most misused words in history. Popular music reflects some of the confusion and misconceptions commonly associated with love. Some songs portray love as a perplexing illusion while others communicate love as being synonymous with sex. Many songs suggest that love is a game with a winner and loser and, of course, someone who gets hurt.

The view that love is something one mysteriously "falls into" and "falls out of" and that there is nothing to learn about it is very common. Such ideas cause unwise mate selection and unsuccessful relationships. Regarding love as something we receive rather than give results in self-centered attitudes that prevent genuine loving relationships.

The thousands of college students enrolled in our classes and the many groups we speak to around the nation report that the type of love they most desire in a marriage relationship is a love that is unconditional and a love that lasts. This type of love is spiritually based and characterizes the successful marriages in our research. Many of these couples reported that the greatest influence on their love relationship is the definition of love described in I Corinthians 13:

> Love is patient, love is kind. It does not envy, it does not boast, it
>   is not proud.
> It is not rude, it is not self-seeking, it is not easily angered,
> it keeps no record of wrong. Love does not delight in evil but
>   rejoices with the truth.
> It always protects, always trusts, always hopes, always perseveres.
> Love never fails . . .[1]

This definition has also influenced many scholars, psychologists, and psychiatrists in their conceptions of love.

Psychotherapist, Erich Fromm, in his classic book, *The Art of Loving*[2], states that love is an art and, as any art, must be practiced and developed. According to Fromm, there are five major components of love.

CARE

We are concerned about the persons we love, wishing to promote their welfare and happiness. Caring means wanting the best for your spouse and wanting him or her to develop in a positive manner. It is caring enough to take the time to listen to your partner even when you don't feel like it.

RESPONSIBILITY

Love is behaving responsibly toward others. We do not hurt those we love by acting irresponsibly. This responsibility is voluntary and involves becoming sensitive to the needs of your spouse and being responsive to those needs.

RESPECT

A basic component of love is respect. Some couples show less respect for each other than for anyone else. The successful couples in our Marriage Success Research Project demonstrated a high degree of mutual respect.

The Greek root of the word respect means "to look at." Respect involves looking at your partner closely enough to be aware of his or her needs and feelings. It communicates an interest in the other person and accepts him or her as a unique individual.

KNOWLEDGE

We gain an awareness of the needs, values, goals, and feelings of the person we love. With this knowledge comes an understanding of the loved one.

We can know a spouse on a superficial level or we can know a

partner more deeply. We may know that a spouse is irritable and
moody. On a deeper level we can know the irritability is the result of
pressures at work and getting too little sleep.

Successful couples invest the time and effort to develop a knowledge and understanding of each other. It is a continuing process and
is viewed by these couples as an adventure.

COMMITMENT

Love is much more than a strong emotional attraction. It is more
than feelings. As Erich Fromm indicates, feelings fluctuate and by
themselves are not a dependable basis for a stable relationship. Ask
any couple who have been married for very long and they will tell you
that there are times when they like each other very much and other
times when they don't.

Love involves making a conscious decision to be committed to a
partner over time in an enduring relationship. Commitment means
promoting the welfare, happiness, and growth of each other. This is
vital to the growth of trust and security in the relationship.

The behavior of love can be learned and can create a powerful
spiritual environment within which the marriage relationship may
prosper and grow. Any couple, regardless of how happy the marriage,
can develop a greater love in their relationship. You can enhance your
marriage relationship by cultivating and practicing loving responses
of care, responsibility, respect, knowledge, and commitment toward
each other.

PATIENCE

Patience is another spiritual value that is important for marriage
success. Happily married couples are patient with each other and
with themselves. Unhappily married couples are much more likely to
be impatient with each other. In fact, some interesting research
evidence indicates that unhappily married individuals tend to
perceive their spouses as being impatient[3]. In the eloquent and

profound definition of love found in I Corinthians 13, one of the first specific behaviors associated with love is patience.

"It took me seven years to get my masters degree," said Lyle. "I even had to get an extension of time from the university. It was so hard working full time and finding time to study and do the research papers well enough to get good grades. I would get very tired and often didn't feel like going out or doing anything fun with Patsy. With school expenses we just didn't have much money so Patsy had to do without a lot of things she wanted.

"I felt bad about all of that for her," said Lyle. "The worst thing is it took me so long to finish. I became very frustrated and almost dropped out of the program twice. But Patsy encouraged me and persuaded me to stay with it. She would tell me I was doing good and remind me of how much progress I had made.

"Patsy was an angel," said Lyle. "I know many women would have become angry and resentful. She was very patient and supportive of me even when I became impatient and frustrated with the situation. I love her for that. I am a lucky man to share my life with her."

Patience is such an important ingredient in marriage success because it reflects love. When you are patient with your partner it makes him or her feel loved and in turn generates feelings of love toward you.

Another basic reason that patience promotes marriage success is that it communicates a commitment. Behavior that is patient sends a message that makes you feel, "My spouse is for me and continues to love me in spite of my shortcomings and my mistakes." In contrast, behavior that is impatient which may be communicated by body language or words, sends a message that makes you feel, "My spouse is getting irritated with me and thinks I am stupid. I am failing. I better try harder or my spouse may leave."

These two messages communicated by patience – love and commitment – and the feelings they generate make a tremendous difference in the quality of a marriage relationship. The practice of patience removes the sense of threat from a relationship. It reduces tension and conflict. Great power comes from the virtue of patience.

Arianne describes a difficult time in her life and the way her husband responded to her. "It was the most unhappy time of my life. My mother had developed Alzheimer's.

"It was so painful to me to be losing my mother as I had always known her," said Arianne. "Mother had gotten to the point where she did not know who I was much of the time. We had to restrain her activity for her own safety.

"I am an only child so I did all the caretaking. Fortunately my husband was a big help. I was emotionally and physically exhausted," she shared. "I was grumpy quite often and was depressed. I know I was not pleasant to be around. I certainly did not feel desirable or attractive.

"I don't know how Lamonte put up with it, but he hung in there. He was so patient with me," she said. "When I was grouchy he just overlooked it. He encouraged me during my periods of depression. Sometimes he didn't say a word; he just held me while I cried. And he did a great deal to help mother. He might take her for a drive or sit out in the swing and talk about old movies. She loved both of those. He was a bright light to me during a dark time."

Patience also serves to increase marriage satisfaction by reducing stress and irritation. When we are impatient we create stress and dissatisfaction in a spouse and in ourselves. Impatience can reduce self-esteem, making a partner feel inadequate.

Some people seem to be impatient by nature. Such a person may say, "That is just the way I am. I have always been like that. I can't change." But you can change. Patience can be developed.

"I was a very impatient person," confessed Rosie. "I was demanding and would be outraged when people did not meet my expectations. And I let them know how I felt. This caused problems in my marriage.

"My husband, fortunately, is a very kind man," she said. "But it got to the point where he could not deal with it. One day he said we had to change something, and maybe we needed to see a marriage counselor. There were things we each needed to change, of course. Fortunately, we were both willing to make those changes because we really loved each other and we were both committed to the marriage.

"I began to see that my impatience was creating misery for both of us," she said. "The counselor helped me to understand that I had learned to be impatient in childhood partly because my mother was very impatient. But the good news was I could learn to be patient.

"It took time – and patience!" Rosie laughed. "But I learned the art of patience. I would remind myself daily that people have different temperaments, different energy levels, different ways of thinking. My way was not necessarily the best way. I also told myself each day that so many things I would get upset about were not really very important."

FAITHFULNESS

The successful couples in our research demonstrated over and over a powerful quality that contributes to their happiness. It also explains why the frustrations and disappointments that result in many couples throwing up their hands and quitting do not threaten these successful couples. This important quality is called faithfulness.

It is a spiritual trait that has different dimensions. One facet of faithfulness is commitment – a theme we have heard repeatedly. A couple who are highly committed to each other can overcome just about anything because they live a message that says, "You are important to me. I will love and care for you in good times and bad times, when we have money and when we are broke, when you are young and when you are old, when you are healthy and when you are sick."

Another dimension of faithfulness is sometimes overlooked, yet it is one of the major reasons why some couples are successful and others are not. This aspect of faithfulness to which we refer is perseverance or determination. It is fastidiousness. It is the quality of sticking to something until the goal is accomplished. It is not giving up.

We all know that it takes determination to succeed in a job, in school, in athletics, or in mastering a musical instrument. However, many couples fail to realize the importance of determination in a successful marriage.

Most of the marriages that fail could have succeeded if the couple had shown the determination to work out problems or even to be willing to address their problems. Most of the problems that result in divorce can be solved and overcome. It is unfortunate that so many couples give up on each other and their marriage when success is within their grasp.

This aspect of faithfulness is typical of the happy couples in our Marriage Success Research Project. They do not give up on each other or the marriage. They don't faint when difficulties or frustrations come. The spirit with which they approach problems is, "We will find a way to solve the problems. We will get through the tough times." The marriage of Catherine and Daniel illustrates the power of faithfulness.

In the first three years of their marriage, Catherine and Daniel had extreme financial hardships. Daniel had completed his bachelor's degree but could not find a job in his field. As a result, he decided to go back for a master's degree in another area which offered more job opportunities. Catherine postponed completing her college degree in order to work full-time to support Daniel going to school.

"As the bumper sticker says, we were 'too broke to pay attention,'" said Catherine. "We were both working in restaurant jobs. The conditions were not good and the hours were long. We were exhausted most of the time and still never had enough money.

"There were many periods when we felt very discouraged," she continued. "We did not have enough money for Daniel to go to school full time so his program took longer.

"Daniel's job was in the kitchen as a cook. He was overqualified for what he was doing. He often wondered what good it had done him to get a college degree. He felt he should be doing a better job of supporting us. But that was discouragement talking. He was doing a great job considering he was going to school, too. We kept reminding ourselves it would not be this way forever.

"In spite of the bad circumstance we managed to have good times," Catherine shared. "We became very good at creating cheap entertainment for ourselves. In fact, some of our happiest memories are from that time of our marriage.

"We did not give in to discouragement. We never gave up," said Catherine. "We had faith things would get better. I'm convinced that Daniel and I became closer for going through those tough times together. We learned to work together and depend on each other.

"It's interesting," Catherine mused. "At the time Daniel believed that working in the restaurant was a waste of his time. But it wasn't. He is now a successful manager of a large number of people. He says the most valuable lessons about business organizations and management he learned working in the restaurant. Today he is grateful for that experience."

Many couples in Catherine and Daniel's situation would have given up. They would have taken their frustrations out on each other and indulged in blaming and hostility. In contrast, Catherine and Daniel made good things happen from difficult circumstances. They strengthened the bonds of their relationship. They did this by using the powerful principle of faithfulness.

PEACE

We live in a hectic, busy, and stressful world. When we allow that hectic, stressful atmosphere to infect our marriage relationships, we become more agitated, busy, and hurried in the way we interact with our spouses.

Your marriage can be greatly enriched by your spiritual faith through the sense of peace that it generates. This is the experience that is shared by many happy couples with long-term marriages, such as Ellen and Lewis. Ellen and Lewis have been happily married for 36 years in spite of the fact they have been through some very rough times.

"The hardest time in our life together was when we were in our late 30's," Lewis stated. "We had one teenager and two school-age children, a house, and dog. You know, the typical family.

"I, however, was in a bottomless pit in my career," said Lewis. "I had not enjoyed if for years. I probably was really not well-suited for it. It's a long story.

"The final straw was a new and difficult boss that I just could not get along with at all. That triggered a decision I had been moving toward for some time," continued Lewis.

"I came home one evening and announced to Ellen that I had resigned my position," Lewis stated. "She was in shock. She asked me if it might have been wise to find another job before quitting the one I had.

"She knew how unhappy I was in that job. I just could not bear to be in that situation any longer," said Lewis. "Ellen bravely assured me we would get through the situation and that I would certainly find a better job.

"But Ellen felt panic and sick at her stomach. And so did I," said Lewis. "There we were – I had resigned my position and I had no job prospects. We had bills to pay and three children depending on us.

"We went through periods of real fear. What would we do? What if we lost everything?

"The most important thing we did was to get down on our knees and pray about it," said Lewis. "We asked for divine guidance and we placed our situation in God's hands.

"We began to feel a great sense of peace in this uncomfortable situation just by knowing that we were not alone and that God would help us," said Lewis. "Reading the Bible together daily was a great source of strength and peace."

Isaiah 41:10 was so helpful to Lewis and Ellen that they repeated it a number of times each day. This powerful scripture reads:

"So do not fear, for I am with you; do not be dismayed, for I am your God. I will strengthen you and help you; I will uphold you with my righteous right hand."[4]

"We allowed this great promise to sink into our minds," said Lewis, "and it had a calming effect. It also gave us hope."

In time, Lewis found a new job which he enjoyed very much. Their income was less for a couple of years, but they made some adjustments. They moved to a smaller house and sold one of their cars. They budgeted very carefully. The children were helpful and cooperative. They all pulled together.

Many of the successful couples shared that they internalize certain passages from the Bible that help them to maintain a sense of peace in their lives. One of the most frequently reported is Psalms 27:1.

"The Lord is my light and my salvation; whom shall I fear? The Lord is the stronghold of my life, of whom shall I be afraid?"[5]

Other thoughts and life philosophies which the successful couples reported helping them to cultivate a serenity in their lives include the following:

"Most of the things we worry about are either in the past (which we can't do anything about) or in the future (most of which never come to pass). So we may as well relax and concentrate on the few things in the present that we can do something about."

"I will do my best and not worry about the rest."

"I cannot do everything. The world does not rest on my shoulders. Another with much stronger shoulders is in control."

"God is bigger than any problem I have."

The Serenity Prayer has helped millions to cope with problems and to reduce anxiety.

God, grant me the serenity

To accept the things I cannot change;

Courage to change the things I can;

And wisdom to know the difference.

Our successful couples take the initiative and do specific things to create a peaceful environment in their marriage relationship. They cultivate certain traditions and activities designed to accomplish this goal.

"We take a walk every evening," shares Matt. "It is good exercise and very relaxing. It gets us away from the telephone and other distractions. It creates a feeling of peacefulness that lasts the rest of the day. These daily walks are a great benefit to our marriage because they help us to relax so that we can really enjoy being together."

A Georgia couple describe a very different tradition that has been an important part of their marriage for many years.

"We read poetry together each evening," the wife shared. "We also enjoy reading a mystery novel to each other."

Many couples reported doing devotionals together. "Reading the Bible together in the evening gives us more confidence and peace and helps us to treat each other better," said one couple.

FORGIVING

It was a rocky road for Emma and Steve in their first three years of marriage. Emma had reason for disappointment and resentment. The bills were being paid and they had food on the table only because of her. Through her hard work and success at her job, she was their sole source of support.

After their wedding, Steve had continued to behave as though he were still single, spending three or four nights a week out with his friends. Their usual recreation was cruising the bars, drinking, and playing pool. Steve gradually slipped into alcoholism and could not keep a job. His nights and days were turned around. He was up most of the night and would sleep during the day.

During the second year of their marriage, Steve became involved in an affair with a woman he had met at a bar. Emma felt deeply hurt and betrayed. She felt she was at the end of her rope, but somehow she held on. She consistently drew on her spiritual resources to forgive him. She tenaciously affirmed that the potential she had seen in him before marriage was the real truth about Steve.

Emma confronted Steve about their life together. She spoke with love and willingness to forgive, but with expectations for change. Steve looked down the road his life was taking and did not like what he saw.

Steve realized Emma had been pushed to the limit and knew that if he continued the affair it would destroy his marriage. He did not want to lose Emma. So he ended the affair.

He also realized that continued alcohol use would eventually destroy every aspect of his life – his ability to earn income, his emotions, his health, and his marriage. Steve had always possessed a great deal of determination and he was a very stubborn man. It served him well in this situation.

Steve did what few people do. He successfully overcame his alcoholism without any professional help. He got a job in sales and did very well. He was persuasive, enthusiastic, personable, and had a natural ability to talk with people. He became the regional sales manager with his company in just a few years. His marriage with Emma grew in happiness and strength. A daughter was born to them. They are very loving and attentive parents.

This positive turn of events in their marriage and in their individual lives took place in large part because of Emma's ability to forgive and her determination to see the potential in Steve when it looked to everyone else as though no potential existed. To forgive is powerful in the effects it has on our lives.

The ability to forgive is a major quality of couples who enjoy a high degree of marriage success. The successful couples in our research were able to forgive each other and themselves. They were able to forgive major wrongs or hurts. These couples also demonstrate a remarkable ability to forgive the little things and to overlook the petty, irritating behavior of each other.

The inability to forgive can destroy relationships as well as emotional health. Research evidence indicates that marriage partners who are unhappy are much more likely to describe a spouse as being unforgiving than are individuals who are happy in their marriage.[6]

It is difficult to forgive when we are hurt or wronged by another person. It is particularly difficult when the hurt or wrong is from a spouse. Following are just a few examples of "hurts" experienced in many marriages.

"My wife took all of our savings out and lost it on one big gambling spree. She did this without my knowledge, of course."

"He is physically abusive to me and the kids. He hit me so hard he broke my nose. That was when I called the police".

"She abandoned me and the kids for two months. She wants to come back now. I don't know if I can take her back."

"I just found out he has financial assets that he has kept secret from me for the past eleven years. I can't believe this. It's like I'm not even a part of his life."

An affair is one of the greatest threats to a marriage. It is also one of the hardest things in life to forgive. Perhaps this is because it is such a deep betrayal of trust and because it involves an area of life in which our self-esteem is most vulnerable.

Whatever the wrong or hurt we have received from a loved one, it can be difficult to deal with, especially when the hurt is deep and the betrayal is great. Yet, the ability to forgive the "unforgivable" is critical to your mental health and to the success of your marriage relationship. So how can this be done?

The successful couples that we interviewed shared six tangible steps that have helped them truly to forgive major hurts as well as minor wrongs. They reported that their spiritual faith was most important in helping them to successfully utilize this six-step formula for forgiveness.

DRAWING ON THE STRENGTH OF GOD

"There have been times when I have been hurt so bad and my anger and hate were so great that I knew if I didn't let it go I would go crazy," said one midwestern wife. "But my feelings were so intense I knew I could not let it go by myself. I knew I must have help from someone else. So I asked God to help me to forgive."

This woman gave us more insight into how she was able to forgive. "In my prayers I confided to God that I didn't think I was capable of forgiving and letting this hurt go.

"I continued my prayers by saying that while I might not be able to forgive, God certainly could. I acknowledged that God had the power to help me to forgive. I then placed this hurt in God's hands and trusted that the great power of God would forgive this person who had hurt me. I asked for the grace and strength to forgive and move on.

"My prayers were answered," she said. "I gradually came to the point of genuinely forgiving and the bad feelings eventually drifted away. A great burden was lifted and I had a new lease on life. But the most important step for me was drawing on the strength of God for the ability to forgive."

REALIZING THE CONSEQUENCES IF YOU DON'T FORGIVE

Jared, a businessman in South Dakota, shared with us a betrayal that led to his bankruptcy and very deep resentment.

"This friend of mine had, at my insistence, become the manager of my clothing store," he said. "He was smart and creative – a big asset. The fact that he was my friend made me trust him completely and I gave him more and more responsibility.

"Everything was going fine for a couple years," he said. "Then the store began losing money. Business quickly got worse. One day my friend disappeared. After a thorough investigation, I discovered he had for some time been taking my merchandise and selling it for himself. When he left he had taken a lot of money with him. The store never recovered from those losses and I was forced to file bankruptcy."

Jared was devastated and feared for his family's security and well-being. All because a friend had betrayed him.

"Feelings of betrayal, anger, and hate consumed me. It changed my personality. I rarely smiled. I became very moody and distant with my wife and children."

This changed for Jared on a cold January night. The kids had gone to bed. Jared and his wife, Carol, were sitting in front of the fireplace watching the changing colors of the fire and listening to the cracking sounds of the burning wood. Finally, she spoke.

"Jared, this hate is slowly killing you. You must forgive and get on with your life."

"I can't forgive what he did to us." Jared quickly responded.

"You can't afford not to forgive," Carol replied. "Look at what this is doing to you. You have become bitter. You are unhappy and you have drawn away from the people who love you the most – me and the children."

Carol's words had a big impact on Jared. "After thinking about what she said, I realized that she was right", said Jared. "I needed to forgive and let this go for my own good if for no other reason. The cost of not forgiving was too great and too destructive.

"Coming to this realization was a turning point for me," said Jared. "I now had a strong motivation to forgive – self-protection. From that time I was able to start forgiving. Now those destructive feelings are gone and no longer have any hold on me."

Jared, with the help of his wife, Carol, discovered the truth of the old proverb, "Hate destroys the container first." Realizing the consequences of not forgiving is an important principle that has helped many to successfully forgive.

EXPRESSING FEELINGS

When Jan's mother died Jan went into an extreme depression. The depression was not only because of the loss of her mother but also because of unfinished business. She had long harbored feelings of resentment toward her mother because she believed her mother had always favored her sister and had given her sister more benefits and advantages.

"My mother's death brought feelings and memories to the surface," said Jan. "Suddenly I had a mixture of strong emotions I was experiencing at the same time – love for my mother, remorse and loss, and resentment.

"I was an emotional mess for months," said Jan. I had never talked with anyone about the resentment I felt toward my mother.

"I reached a point where I felt if I didn't talk with someone about this I would explode," she said. "Finally, I shared the resentful feeling toward my mother with Rex, my husband. Rex is a good listener. And I poured out my heart to him. I told him everything – all the ways my mother would favor my sister and how it made me feel."

"I felt so much better after I shared all of this with Rex," said Jan.

"It was therapeutic. He may never know how much he helped me by just listening and being concerned. This was the first time I had expressed those feelings with anyone. This helped to get me to the point where I could forgive and let the hurt and bad feelings go."

Jan's experience represents an important step on the pathway of forgiving. Simply talking and sharing our feelings about a hurt or wrong with someone we trust can indeed be therapeutic.

Sometimes it can be helpful to talk with the person who has hurt or wronged us. This can give the other person an understanding of how their actions have affected us. It may give us better understanding, also for sometimes we learn that it was not the intention of the other person to hurt us. Even in those instances where the hurtful act was intentional, our talking with the other person can provide a needed release and give a sense of closure about the matter.

REMEMBER THAT WE HAVE ALL MADE MISTAKES

The husband sat in stony silence in the counselor's office glaring at his wife. She pleaded with him again to forgive her. She assured him that she had made a bad mistake, that it would never happen again, and that she loved him more than anything.

He told her that he could never forgive her for having an affair and that he would never be able to trust her again. He then repeated his position that the only solution for them was to divorce.

While there were some problems in their relationship that needed to be corrected, these two people had enjoyed a basically good marriage for several years. Their marriage was savable. Not only was it savable, their relationship had the potential to become stronger and happier. The major obstacle to this happening was the husband's inability to forgive his wife.

As the counseling sessions progressed it came out that the husband had been involved in an affair earlier in their marriage.

Counselor: How did your wife react to your affair?

Husband: She was very upset

Counselor: How did your marriage survive your having an affair?

Husband: I stopped the affair.

Counselor: Was that the only reason?

Husband: She forgave me.

Counselor: Were you glad she forgave you?

Husband: Yes.

Counselor: Is there a reason why your affair was so different from her affair that she could forgive you but now you cannot forgive her?

There was not an immediate answer to the counselor's last question. The husband silently wrestled with these questions for a time.

A couple of sessions later the husband spoke up, "You know I have thought a lot about your question of why my affair was so different from her affair that she could forgive me but I could not forgive her."

"Of course there is no reason," he said. He turned to his wife and said, "If you had not forgiven me our marriage would have been over a long time ago."

"I want our marriage to continue," he said. "It is more important than any of the mistakes that either of us makes."

"I forgive you," he continued, "I thank you that you forgave me years ago. It may take me a while to work through some of these feelings. But I will. I'm going to be a better husband and we're going to have a better marriage."

Indeed, their marriage relationship did become stronger and happier than ever before. This happened because they recommitted to their marriage and because the husband was able to forgive.

The step that was critical in this husband being able to forgive was being reminded of a wrong action he had taken for which he had been forgiven. It is far easier to forgive when we remember that we are not perfect, that we make mistakes, and that we have wronged others.

LETTING IT GO

"I didn't know how to really forgive until I was 50 years old," said one North Carolina woman. "I would say the words, 'I forgive'. But I would keep thinking about the wrong I had suffered. I would keep replaying the particular incident in my mind until I just felt sick. I guess I was expert at hanging on to the bad feelings."

A Viet Nam veteran shares that he suffered post traumatic stress disorder for 25 years. "I was in and out of residential treatment all those years but remained emotionally sick," he said. "I stayed sick because I kept reliving the horrible things that happened during the war. I kept them so close to me that I had nightmares about the war at least once a week. I was still angry and I had not forgiven others or myself for things that had happened during the war.

"In one of the group sessions I heard the group therapist say something he had probably said many times before. But this time I heard it. Maybe I was ready for it. He said, 'When you guys are ready, you will let these bad memories and experiences go. You're not ready yet but when you are, you'll leave these unhappy memories and feelings behind.'

"I remember thinking I was ready to change. It was time. I had spent 25 years making myself sick and the lives of my wife and children difficult by hanging on to these horrible things from the past that I could do nothing about.

"But I could choose to stop hanging on to those memories that were making me sick," he said. "I made the decision to do just that, and I decided to forgive others and myself for the horrible things that had happened. With my decision and the help of the therapist and my wife, and most of all with the help of God, I was successful in letting go of those memories that had been making me sick. I was finally able to forgive. The real healing then took place. It did not happen overnight. I had to gradually learn new thought patterns. But it happened."

Many have found the use of symbolism very helpful in letting go of resentment and hurt. For example, the Viet Nam war veteran describes an action that was helpful to him. "I took several sheets of paper and wrote on each one such words as Viet Nam, fear, pain, horror, anger – all of the feelings I had been harboring. I then took the sheets of paper along with a couple of movie videos about Viet Nam into the middle of a large field and burned them. As I watched the fire burn I said out loud, 'I am letting it go for good.' That simple act helped me to feel I was finished with it.

A Georgia woman shared a deep resentment she held toward her father in-law for years for some very hurtful things he had done to her and to her husband. "I continued to resent him for years after he died," she said. "I knew for my own health I needed to forgive and move on. Fortunately I eventually did something that helped me to accomplish that goal.

"I visited his grave alone and just talked to him as though he were there. I mentioned the things he had done that had hurt me and his son. I described my feelings. When I was finished I told him that I forgave him," she said. "I then said I am now letting all this resentment, anger, and hurt feelings go. I am through with them and am not going to let them bother me any more. When I walked away from his grave I felt at peace," she said. "I no longer felt resentful or angry."

Many of the successfully married husbands and wives in our study reported using a technique described by a Missouri woman. "I write a letter to the person who has wronged me," she said. "I tell them what they did that hurt me and how it has made me feel. Instead of mailing the letter I tear it into pieces and drop it in the waste basket. I forgive the person and as the torn pieces fall into the waste basket, I visualize my hurt falling into the waste basket also. It really helps me to release the whole thing."

REPLACING THE NEGATIVE EMOTIONS

Letting the negative feelings go is an essential part of the process of forgiveness. When the negative feelings are released a void is left in us. If the void is not filled it is easier for the resentment and hate to return. The final step in the road to forgiving is to fill the void with something powerful and good. The negative emotions must be replaced by positive emotions of love, hope, and peace.

Geneva and Randall's 14-year-old son was shot in a drive-by shooting. It was random. He did not know his assailants. He was left paralyzed by the shooting. "This was the worst experience we had ever been through, said Geneva. "The hurt, the grief, the fear and the anger were overwhelming."

The experience seemed to have a more destructive impact on Geneva. "I had a lot of hate and anger. It took me a long time to even think about forgiving," she said. "When I finally thought I had put this behind me the hate and the anger would return. I kept coming back to the same feeling. Their mean, stupid, violent act, had left my child paralyzed and I hated them for it."

Her hate and resentment was taking a toll on Geneva's health. It was also having a negative impact on her marriage relationship and on her relationship with her son. "One day Randall said to me, ' we want you back, Geneva. We need you but you don't seem to be with us. Your mind is somewhere else."

"This blew me away," said Geneva. "It scared me. But I realized he was right. I had been pulling away from the two people I loved most in the world. I had been putting so much energy and time into hate and resenting the terrible thing that happened that there was nothing left for them or anyone else."

"I could not talk to Randall at that moment," said Geneva. "I went into our bedroom, threw myself on the bed and cried for what seemed like hours. I felt exhausted, but strangely better afterwards," Geneva said. "It was as though I had released something that I desperately needed to release.

"I began to think about how thankful I was to have Randall and our son, Bobby. I thanked God for the first time that Bobby's life had been spared in that shooting. Randall was right," Geneva said. "They did need me. This experience had been horrible for them, too. I had not been thinking about them. I was too obsessed with my own hurt."

Geneva made a commitment to change her life. The focus of her thoughts shifted from the hurt to the love of her family. "I dedicated my life each day to giving Randall and Bobby all of my love," Geneva shared. "I made it my daily goal to spend time with them to listen to them, to help them. I looked for ways to bring happiness into their lives."

Gradually the hate, hurt, and resentment faded away. Geneva was finally able to genuinely forgive and really let go of the destructive feelings because she had replaced them with something more powerful – love.

CREATING JOY

The happy couples in our national Marriage Success Research Project express love and appreciation for one another by providing pleasurable, joyful experiences for each other. Is it any wonder they are happy? This relationship pattern is profound. Too many couples either provide little or no pleasurable experiences for each other or they provide primarily unpleasant experiences.

The impact of this simple approach has been underestimated and, as a result, is practiced little. There are many ways in which couples can increase daily pleasure and happiness for each other. We will now look at four broad categories by which couples may approach this endeavor.

JOYFUL HAPPENINGS

Creating a joyful happening is one way of bringing happiness into a marriage relationship. Dr. Herbert Otto, author of **More Joy in Your Marriage**[7], published by Hawthorn Books, suggests that there are too few joyful happenings in our daily lives and that we can remedy this by planning more of them. The successful couples in our research are skilled at applying this principle.

"Tesney completely surprised me last month with a party," said a Maryland husband. She invited only people that are my good friends and she planned some activities that I really enjoy. Everybody had fun. It was a total surprise to me and I loved it."

Other examples of joyful happenings are a trip to the mountains, a fun game of scrabble, or simply a much needed and desired evening of relaxation at home. A joyful happening can be anything that brings enjoyment and happiness. It is made more special by one partner caring enough to create the happy experience for the other.

THIS IS YOUR DAY

"This is your day" is a simple and enjoyable practice in which on a certain day the husband does everything in his power to make his wife feel happy and special. Then on another day the wife does everything in her power to create a day of happiness for him.

Whatever pleases that partner is the appropriate behavior for the day. This might include cooking a favorite food, breakfast in bed, going to a concert, or throwing a surprise party. As one Texas woman said, "I like to think of myself as a genie who fulfills my husband's every wish and who prepares surprises and activities to add to the fun and beauty of the day."

Some couples like to have "this is your day" for each other once a month. However frequently it is practiced, it brings a lot of joy. As Dr. Herbert Otto states the harder one partner tries to make this day truly one of joy for the other, the more likely the other will want to give that partner the same kind of experience. What a great relationship pattern – each partner planning creative ways to make each other happy!

LOVE GIFTS

The use of love gifts is a practice that many couples have found to be particularly fulfilling. A love gift is anything one partner does for another that gives happiness or assistance. A husband's love gift to his wife might include washing dishes for her on a particular day. A wife's gift to her husband might include washing the car or mowing the lawn. Some couples find that trading love gifts on a daily basis is very enjoyable.

"In the early years of our marriage we had very little money," shares an Oklahoma husband. "We never thought of ourselves as poor, but it was impossible for us to exchange the kind of gifts that we would have liked to have given. So we began exchanging love gifts. I remember on Christmas my wife gave me a box of pancake flour with a note that promised she would make pancakes for me each Sunday

– a task she really disliked – for a year. It was another way of saying, 'I love you.'"

"My gifts included pledges to do the household things she disliked," he said. "With the passing of years we continued the love gifts at Christmas. When our children were small they would give a love gift that involved bringing in the newspaper at night or taking out the trash."

"Our love gifts were not limited to members of our family," he continued. "When my son was young, his love gift to his Godmother was to collect pine straw and tie them in little bundles she would use to start fires in her fireplace."

"As the years have passed, the love gifts have meant a great deal to members of my family. Because they frequently involve pledges for an entire year, they are gifts that remind us throughout the year of our love for each other."

DOING WHAT YOU ENJOY

One common pattern we observe among successful couples is that they participate in activities that they like. It is an important way to bring more joy into a marriage relationship. If a couple enjoys playing tennis, then they can have more fun by structuring their schedule so that they play tennis together regularly. If a couple enjoys fishing, they should fish. If there is nothing a couple enjoys more than camping in the mountains, then they should certainly camp in the mountains periodically.

While this may seem to be an obvious principle it is not widely practiced. Many couples do not do the things they find fun because they feel they are too busy or because they have fallen into the habit of "putting off" these fun activities which they may view as frivolous and not of great importance.

In truth, taking the time to do things together that both partners enjoy is a great enrichment to the relationship. Good times spent together is priceless in contributing to the strength of a marriage. Both fresh vitality and interest can be added to a marriage relationship by a couple listing the activities they most enjoy in life, and then following through with plans to actually participate in those activities.

"Marjorie and I listed the five things we most enjoyed doing," said Lyndon. "None of them were a significant part of our active life style. So we tried an experiment," he shared. "For two months we actively participated in our five most enjoyable activities. The vitality this brought into our relationship was amazing," he said. "We both feel younger and more energetic. We are less tense and have rediscovered the art of having fun."

Chapter 11

GIVING THE BLESSING

It is our heartfelt wish that your marriage is a voyage of love, happiness, and joyful adventure. It is our hope that you have smooth sailing and that your ship steers clear of dangerous waters. Should you find your ship being tossed to and fro by a savage storm we want you to know that you have resources you can draw from that will get you through the storm. It is our desire that the husbands and wives represented in this book remain an inspiration and help to you.

There is one additional resource you may take with you on your voyage of marriage intimacy. It is our pleasure to present this to you as a gift at this time. It is most appropriate to present this resource as we conclude this book. This gift is interwoven with the other principles discussed in this book, yet there is something that sets it apart and makes it different.

At first, we as researchers did not understand the nature and extent of this particular phenomenon. Then as we began to understand what we were seeing among these successful couples, it became apparent that it was a prominent characteristic they shared. It is a powerful tool for use by husbands and wives who desire to draw close to each other and experience a more intimate relationship. For those who possess this it is truly a gift – a gift that can transform a life and a marriage. We speak of the gift of the blessing.

The gift of the blessing has been so eloquently discussed by Gary Smalley and John Trent in their book, *The Gift of the Blessing*. They have earned our gratitude by helping us all to better understand this powerful idea.

THE BLESSING FOR THE VOYAGE

The importance of the blessing to the success of a sea voyage has been recognized by sailors throughout history. For example, it was the typical custom during the age of Christopher Columbus that each day a sailor would announce the day by saying:

"Blessed be the light of day and He who sends the night away."

This was followed by the sailors joining together in saying the "Pater Noster" (Our Father) and the "Ave Maria." They would then recite:

"God give us good days, good voyage, good passage to the ship, captain and master and good company, so let there be a good voyage. . ."[1]

The blessing is also important to the voyage of a marriage. Why? It is because of the deep need we each have to be accepted unconditionally and valued. This essentially is what a blessing involves – an act of accepting and valuing another.

Many people never feel that they are truly accepted or highly valued by a spouse. For some this great need has been unmet all of their lives. Unconditional acceptance and high regard were never granted to them by their parents or anyone else.

Nothing is more important to our self-esteem and sense of security than to have someone important in our lives giving us unconditional acceptance. When we are highly valued by another we feel worthy and as though we have something good to give to others. In other words, it makes us feel lovable, and therefore we are better able to give love!

Allysa is a pretty young woman with a sweet personality, yet, she is unhappy in her marriage of three years. She and her husband, Kyle, have just separated. She wants desperately to feel loved and accepted. But Kyle has not been able to satisfy that need.

Allysa's birth was an unwanted one. She felt rejected by her mother throughout her childhood. No accomplishment or behavior ever earned her mother's approval. She never knew her father.

When she married, she looked to Kyle to make her feel lovable. But instead of giving unconditional acceptance and high regard, Kyle soon began to find fault with Allysa – the way she cooked, the new dress she bought, her job. His criticisms grew into ridicule. He was especially skilled in the use of sarcastic "humor" which kept her spirit beat down. Kyle behaved in this manner in large part because he had been treated this way in growing up and he did not feel good about himself.

So their marriage relationship was one in which Kyle withheld the acceptance and high regard that Allysa needed and instead related to her in a way that made her feel inadequate and undesirable. Because she felt unlovable, she was then unable to give Kyle the acceptance and love he needed. Neither had received the blessing.

THE PRACTICE OF THE BLESSING: FIVE PRINCIPLES

The practice of the blessing has been a major way of providing a sense of acceptance throughout history. It has played an important role in Jewish history. In fact, as Gary Smalley and John Trent observe, the word blessing is one of the most important words in the Bible and was used over 640 times in the Old Testament alone.[2] It was recognized as being very powerful and very desirable.

There are four basic relationship principles that have been utilized historically in giving a blessing. Each one of these principles is important for marriage partners to use as they give each other the gift of the blessing. Gary Smalley and John Trent have done an outstanding job of discussing these principles in their wonderful book, *The Gift of the Blessing*, published by Thomas Nelson. We highly recommend their book to you.

Understanding each of these principles will enable you to be more successful in giving your spouse the gift of the blessing. It will also greatly enhance your marriage happiness. Each of these principles will now be discussed. However, we are adding a fifth principle, which will be discussed first. It is closely linked with the other four. The presence of this additional principle promotes the practice of the other four.

THE DECISION TO BE A SOURCE OF BLESSING TO YOUR SPOUSE

Simply making the decision that you are going to be a source of blessing to your mate will have a powerful, transforming effect on the marriage. That decision establishes conditions which make it easier to give the blessing. It creates a positive flow of energy into the relationship.

Why is this one decision so powerful? Certainly it is a clear demonstration of commitment. It shifts the focus of the spouse who decides to be a source of blessing from being irritated by the shortcoming and character flaws of a mate to being concerned with increasing the happiness and quality of life for that spouse. It increases the inclination to reach out to your partner more and to become less self-centered. Making this decision to be a source of blessing to your spouse changes the emphasis from being mostly concerned about whether your needs are being met to an emphasis on meeting the needs of your partner. In making this decision, you have established that love and good intentions will guide your interactions with your mate.

Janie and Charles' marriage was rocky. It had been deteriorating over the past two years to the point that they were considering ending their 12-year marriage. However, their marriage had been good for most of this time together. It was only in the last few years that their relationship began to fall apart. What had happened?

Janie had fallen victim to a depression that developed in part from some unresolved childhood experiences and also from her high-stress career as an executive of a large corporation. Depression and stress fatigued her and she grew quiet and withdrawn; she often went to bed early or wanted to be alone. Charles felt rejected. Her depression also resulted in her becoming more irritable and snappish. Hurt by this pattern of behavior, Charles reacted by becoming irritable and hostile toward Janie.

Their marriage spiraled downward. One evening Charles was visiting with his father and mentioned the apparent wisdom of proceeding with a divorce.

After listening to his son expound on divorce as the logical solution, the father asked, "Is a divorce what you want?"

Charles replied that he did not want a divorce but that there didn't seem to be any hope for the marriage to be saved.

"There is hope if you don't give up," said the father. "You enjoyed ten good years in your marriage. Are you ready to give that up so easily?"

Charles protested that he had tried but that nothing worked and that Janie's behavior was driving him crazy. His father paused a moment and asked, "Charles, have you considered the possibility that her behavior may have little to do with you? She may not be well. Have you thought about the possibility that she may need help from you?"

The question caught Charles by surprise. The truth was he had not been thinking about her needs. He had been preoccupied with his own.

"The more I thought about my Dad's question, the more ashamed I felt," Charles confessed. "I had known for some time that Janie was not acting like herself. But I had been so caught up in my hurt feelings that I neglected to consider what that might mean.

"I sat on Dad's patio late into the night doing some soul

searching. I concluded that our marriage deserved better than my giving up on it," said Charles. "If Janie was sick, there was no need to take her negative behavior so personally. That helped me to look at things differently."

Charles had been trying unsuccessfully to change Janie. He now turned his efforts to something he could do – changing his own behavior.

"I decided to do everything I could to make her happy. There were a lot of little acts of consideration and thoughtfulness I began to do every day – like a surprise bouquet of flowers or having supper ready when she came in on the days she worked later than I did."

Charles did everything he could think of to promote her happiness and well-being. He did not worry about her reactions. At first she seemed a little suspicious and skeptical of his new pattern of behavior. But as his positive interaction toward her continued, she was pleasantly bewildered.

Charles soon began to see a change in Janie. She was less hostile and negative.

"She became less withdrawn," said Charles. "We started to talk again. And we actually enjoyed talking. Because we could talk with each other without getting into screaming matches, we were able to figure out a lot of our problems."

Janie received medical help and assistance from a professional counselor for her depression. She also found another job that was less stressful and less demanding. She made this decision for her own health and the health of her marriage. Their marriage relationship was restored to happiness and satisfaction.

The critical step in saving their marriage and reversing the downward spiral was the decision Charles made to do everything he could to promote Janie's happiness and well-being. He did not realize that he had made the decision to give Janie and their marriage his blessing, but that is exactly what he had done. As he actually gave the blessing to Janie it lifted their relationship from despair to happiness.

TOUCH

Touch was a basic aspect of giving a blessing in Jewish homes. Each time the blessing was bestowed in the Old Testament, touching in the form of kissing, hugging, or the laying on of hands was involved. The human touch communicated genuine caring and accompanied the spoken words of the blessing.

Touch is the most basic form of communication. A large body of research evidence suggests that infants who are deprived of human touch experience more developmental problems, are more irritable, have more eating problems, are more likely to be seriously underweight, are more socially unresponsive, and have a higher infant mortality rate.[3]

Touch is also a basic need in adults and is certainly vital in marriage. A caring touch can enrich the marriage relationship. Not just in the bedroom, but a caring touch is also important in the kitchen, on the way to the grocery store, in the morning before leaving for work. A kiss, holding hands, an encouraging hand on the shoulder, an enthusiastic embrace – all communicate caring, intimacy and affection. Each of these forms of touching sends the important message, "I value you," which is an essential component of the blessing. We need to produce bumper stickers and billboards that read:

"Have you hugged your spouse today?"

Physical touch is a way of connecting with another person. Too many couples lead lives that literally are disconnected from each other. They may rarely embrace, snuggle to watch TV, or hold hands in the movies; not surprisingly, they often feel lonely and yearn for intimacy.

Physical touch is also a symbol – an expression of making connection with your spouse in a larger, more wholistic sense. So when you hug, kiss or hold hands, you are giving an important part of the blessing to your mate. You are making a connection. Of course, the blessing is made more complete when you go beyond the physical touch and also make connection in such ways as being a good listener, showing a genuine interest in your spouse, and making sure that you spend a lot of time together.

THE SPOKEN MESSAGE OF HIGH REGARD

In the ancient Hebrew culture, when a family blessing was given it was accompanied by a spoken message and a communication of high value to the one receiving the blessing. These two aspects of the blessing are closely linked and we will treat them as one here.

Many of the successful couples in our research give these two components of the blessing to each other daily. They value each other highly and they verbally communicate their high regard. This is one of the most important reasons their marriages are successful and their relationships are filled with happiness.

One of the most important needs humans have is the need to be appreciated. We need to feel that we are worth something, that we have something of value to contribute, that there is something special about us, and that we have potential. We want our hard efforts and accomplishments to be acknowledged. We desperately need to feel that we are highly valued by those closest to us. Appreciation is another word for this important component of the blessing – the spoken message of high regard.

For more than 25 years Nick has conducted research with thousands of strong families throughout the nation and the world. The results of this research have revealed that one of the six major qualities which make families strong is the quality of appreciation.[4]

Many spouses are unhappy in their marriage because they withhold this vital part of the blessing from each other. Many children never receive the spoken word of high regard from their parents. The failure to give appreciation can destroy relationships and may destroy emotional health.

In South Africa, Arkansas, and in a few other parts of the world a diamond industry exists. In those places miners spend a lot of time digging for diamonds. They move tons and tons of dirt just to find a few tiny pebbles about the size of your smallest fingertip. However, they don't mind moving all that dirt because they are not focusing on the dirt. Their focus is on finding the diamonds. It is diamonds they're hunting – not dirt!

Yet, too often in our marriages, in the relationship with our children, and in our other human relationships, we are just the opposite. We look for the dirt in each other and ignore the beautiful diamonds that exist within each one of us. We criticize, complain, focus on each other's shortcomings, use sarcasm, and ridicule. And at the same time we either totally ignore the diamonds or deliberately brush the diamonds aside and say in effect, "Now I want to give my complete attention to your failures, your inadequacies. I want to emphasize what I don't like about you and what you need to change."

As we engage in this rather common pattern of behavior, we are withholding the blessing from each other. And something else is taking place. Expressing a pattern of criticism, sarcasm, put-downs, and ridicule has the effect of creating the opposite of the blessing – a curse. It becomes a curse whether it is meant to be or not because it destroys self-esteem, creates hate and resentment, diminishes hope for the relationship, and tears down self-confidence. It creates conditions that prevent intimacy.

One reason that people express appreciation so infrequently is that they're afraid they will be accused of flattery or of being insincere. In truth, your spouse has so many good qualities that all you have to do is look for them and then express genuine appreciation for those qualities. You are not using flattery. You're sincere because those good qualities in your mate are real.

Sometimes people don't give appreciation to others because they themselves don't feel appreciated. Their self-esteem and confidence are low. They feel they have to protect their meager store of well-being. Consequently they can't share appreciation or recognition with others.

Perhaps the most common reason for not expressing appreciation is habit. Many people have simply never learned to express appreciation. The good news is that habits can be changed. Appreciation can be learned and cultivated.

Laticia and Gregory have established a tradition which has helped them develop the habit of appreciation. It has also enriched their marriage.

"This is a dinnertime tradition that we observe once a week," said Laticia. "It's fun and easy to do. It has brought us closer.

"The way it works is that on our special night this week, Gregory will be the honored one. After dinner is over I will pick one specific thing about Gregory that I really like. For example, we've heard a good bit on our news this week about a local man accused of abusing his son. I'm reminded of what a wonderful father Greg is. This time I'll tell him how much it means to me that he is such a good father. I will give him my heartfelt appreciation for spending a lot of his time with the children and for being such a good role model.

"The next week, I will be the honored one," said Laticia, "and he will mention something he really appreciates about me."

This tradition has done two important things for Laticia and Gregory. First, it has helped them to get in the habit of looking for each other's strengths. And second, it has helped them to cultivate the habit of verbally expressing appreciation for those strengths. They have learned to give each other a great blessing – the message of high regard.

Gwen and Boone, on the other hand, were experiencing a high degree of dissatisfaction in their relationship. Their marriage had become a running battle of squabbles, skirmishes, and yelling matches. They blamed, fussed, and criticized on a daily basis.

As a last effort to save the marriage, they decided to go to a marriage counselor. The counselor began by seeing each one individually because of the high levels of antagonism. The counselor did something that proved to be very wise and helpful.

The counselor asked Gwen to take a few minutes and write down on a piece of paper 10 of Boone's good qualities. At first she was irritated at the idea and dismissed the assignment. But the counselor insisted and she finally did it. Gwen admitted she was surprised that she could come up with 10 good qualities.

Gwen was then given another assignment. During the next three weeks she was to use her own words to express sincere appreciation to Boone for each of those 10 good qualities. Unknown to Gwen, Boone had been given the same assignments.

"By the end of the next month, a remarkable change had taken place in our marriage," said Gwen. "I never would have believed it could happen. But the whole tone of our relationship turned more positive and loving."

The positive tone of their relationship grew. Today, they enjoy a strong, happy marriage relationship – something most of their friends would not have thought possible. With the help of the counselor, they were successful in dealing with some other issues that needed to be worked out in their relationship. But a vital step in transforming their marriage relationship was becoming aware of each other's strengths and expressing appreciation for those strengths. Those diamonds were there all along.

"It was almost like we had been hypnotized by what we didn't like in each other and that's all we saw," said Gwen. "So we just got in the habit of criticizing each other. It was like a breath of life when we stopped putting each other down all the time and began to make each other feel good."

Gwen and Boone learned the habit of appreciation. In effect, there was a rebirth of their marriage because they started giving each other the blessing of appreciation.

VISUALIZING A SPECIAL FUTURE

Envisioning a special future for the person being blessed has been a common feature of the blessing as practiced in the ancient Jewish culture. Jewish homes today commonly picture a special future for each of their children.

It makes us feel good to know that someone thinks that we have a good future ahead of us. It is encouraging and gives us a sense of confidence and optimism about the future.

Husbands and wives can give each other a blessing by sharing a positive vision for their marriage. Many couples share no vision and consequently have no sense of purpose or direction for their marriage. One young couple in discussing their upcoming marriage expressed the view that, "Well, if it doesn't work out we can get a divorce." This vision for their marriage is not a hopeful one and is not a vision that engenders a sense of security in either partner.

Many successful couples have a positive vision for their marriage but they never formally state it or write it down. Some couples create a written vision statement for their marriage where they describe the positive directions they wish to see their marriage relationship go. One couple prepared an attractive vision statement for the future of their marriage. They selected a nice wooden frame for it. It hangs prominently on their living room wall and reads:

Today is the first day of the rest of our life together.

Our marriage will be like a tree by the clean, fresh waters of a brook.

Our marriage will prosper and grow strong.

Our marriage will bring joy and enjoy peace.

We will walk hand in hand on life's journey together.

In the storms we will comfort each other. For the challenges we will strengthen each other.

Laughter will be part of our daily diet.

We will bring out the beauty in each other.

We will plant love and harvest joy.

"It was rewarding for us to sit down together and create this vision statement of our marriage," said the wife. "It puts into words very important goals and desires for our life together.

"It has helped us a lot," she said. "We see that vision statement every day, at least a couple of times a day. It makes us feel good to look at it. It reminds us of what our marriage can be. You know, it's interesting our marriage is pretty much like that vision statement."

It is interesting, but not surprising. The vision statement acts as a self-fulfilling prophecy. It is a guide. Most of us tend to act as we think we are expected to act. We are inclined to act in accordance with our own prophecies.

Also, this couple's positive vision for the future of their marriage is encouraging to them. It gives them confidence and optimism about their marriage relationship, which in turn motivates them to respond to each other in positive, supportive ways.

Visualize a special, good future for your marriage. Share this with each other. It may help you to write a vision statement. Or you may choose to renew your wedding vows and include your vision for the future of your marriage in those vows.

However you choose to do it, maintaining a vision of a wonderful future for your marriage can encourage and serve as a guide to help you set desirable goals. It can be a blessing to your marriage. A vision is a powerful force.

At a personal level, what kind of vision do you hold for your marriage partner? It is very important that you have a vision of a positive, special future for your spouse. We communicate our visions for each other by the words we speak, by our judgments, and by our attitudes. We like to be around people who believe in us. We are discouraged by those who don't believe in us and often we try to avoid them. This is due in part to an underlying principle of human behavior that we tend to see ourselves as we think others see us.

Dennis is a top executive in a computer corporation. His position requires that he host social functions in his home. His wife, Ruby, is called upon to play a major role in hosting these receptions and dinners. She is not comfortable in large groups and does not especially enjoy entertaining this way. She enjoys it even less because of Dennis' criticisms. He is frustrated by what he considers to be her social ineptness. He often goes on a tirade following one of these social events and blasts her with such criticisms as:

"I wish you could learn to mingle with the guests better. I don't think you said one word to some of the people here tonight.

"Can't you show any interest in people? They will think you are unfriendly.

"I think you are afraid of being around people."

Dennis' badgering and criticism are hurting Ruby's self-esteem and confidence. His words are sending the messages that he has little faith in her, and that she is a failure, and that she has no special future.

His words are also hurting their marriage relationship by building resentment in Ruby. Her hurt and anger are growing because he is making her feel inadequate.

The vision Dennis holds of Ruby as a person has limited her future. His negative attitudes have built a wall around her in his own mind, and perhaps in her mind as well. This wall imprisons her and prevents her from becoming different than what his judgments have proclaimed her to be. The wall is preventing her from claiming a positive, successful future.

In a very real sense Dennis has withheld the blessing from Ruby. Instead, his behavior has placed a curse on her and their marriage.

In contrast, consider the case of Ward. Ward enjoyed a successful, thriving business of his own. He had a wonderful wife, three adorable children, and an accepted place in the community. Then came a problem that got out of control – addiction to pain medications after a back injury. Heavy fines and a mandatory prison sentence followed his third arrest for DUI. The business was lost. Most of his friends abandoned him. His reputation was ruined. Devastated, he was sure he had lost everything. He thought about committing suicide, but did not.

Instead, Ward has bounced back. He is now drug free. Shortly after being released from prison he began rebuilding his own business.

When Ward was asked what had been responsible for his recovery he replied, "Renewing my spiritual faith and drawing closer to God was most important. Going through a good drug rehabilitation program certainly played a major role."

He hesitated. His voice cracked a little as he continued. "I can't find the words to tell you what a life saver my wife has been throughout this situation.

"I think God was operating through her," he said. "She was the main reason I didn't give up and kill myself.

"She was there with me the whole time," he said. "She visited me in prison as often as possible. She sent letters which always included an uplifting thought.

"She never gave up on me. She did not see me as an addict or a criminal like so many other people did. Technically, I was those things. But she looked beyond that and saw I was more.

"She would talk with me about ideas for starting a new business when I got out of prison. She would remind me that I was a good businessman and talk about how creative I was. She often mentioned that people really enjoyed working for me because I treated them good. She made me feel like I could do anything."

Ward's optimism about the future grew because his wife believed in him and she presented a vision of a good future for him. Her vision of a bright future for Ward was communicated often by dwelling on his strengths and his potential rather than harping on his mistakes.

COMMITMENT

The final component in giving the blessing is commitment. Ward's wife is a shining example of commitment. She stayed with him. She did not give up on him. She communicated high regard and a vision of a positive future for Ward in spite of his mistakes and in spite of the fact that his behavior did not merit her respect. Her attitude and commitment not only helped bring him through a very difficult and dangerous time in his life. It also brought out the best in Ward. This is the beauty and the power of commitment.

Commitment is interwoven with other aspects of giving the blessing. Commitment is carrying through – making the effort and taking the time to bestow the blessing upon your spouse.

Commitment is making your marriage relationship a top priority with respect to how you invest your time and energy. Many couples find their commitment and their happiness eroded by misplaced priorities.

As is true for many couples, Lindy and Derrick's marriage was being overwhelmed by pressure and demands. Their time together was being stolen away by other things.

"We were involved in too many activities," said Derrick. "We had time for everything else – for work, for volunteer efforts, for friends. But no time for each other!

"It was stupid to have a priority system that put our marriage relationship on the back burner, robbed us of happiness and created stress," he said. "We committed ourselves to changing our priorities.

"We dropped some of our community involvement and brought less work home," Derrick continued. "We put our marriage on the front burner. We spent more time talking to each other every day. We started eating every evening meal together – no exceptions. We now go out on a fun 'date' at least twice a month.

"These changes may sound simple," Derrick said. "But they have made a world of difference for us. We are much happier and far less stressed out."

This couple is happier and more relaxed because of their commitment – their decision – to make their marriage a top priority concerning the way they invest their time and energy. They committed to bless their marriage relationship and each other.

An important characteristic of the successful couples in the Marriage Success Research Project is their commitment to each other for the long haul. They expect their marriages to endure.

When they encounter an unhappy or tough period in their marriage they don't have to make the decision of whether they will stay together or not. They have already made the decision to love each other in good times as well as in bad times. The commitment to be there and not abandon each other is a foundation of marriage. Commitment says, "We will do whatever it takes to love and bless each other."

Few things are as important in building a satisfying marriage relationship as the sincere commitment of one partner to the other. Knowing that your spouse is completely committed to you gives a sense of belonging and security. It increases self-esteem and makes you feel special. You can trust a partner to do right by you. In this way commitment is a blessing and contributes to marriage happiness.

"I know Mack is 100 percent for me," said Angelita. "That's what I cherish most about him.

"He shows his commitment in many ways. And I try to be just as committed to him," she continued. "There is one example I want to share with you.

"Our children were young – ages six and four when it happened. We lived in a rural area and the nearest house was about a half-mile away.

"My husband had returned home from a trip at about midnight and found the house on fire. The children were standing in the front yard crying. Fortunately, they had wakened and gotten out the window. Of course, they had not been able to call anyone so there was no fire truck on the way.

"My husband came into the house through the flames and smoke. He burst into our bedroom and somehow managed to get me out of the house.

"He suffered some severe burns and some lung damage. He could have been killed. He risked his life to save mine. Obviously, if he had not put his life on the line I would not be here today.

"It's kind of funny that through the years when I get aggravated at Mack about something I often think about this incident and the aggravation just fades away."

What a powerful blessing couples give to each other when they communicate this 100 percent commitment such as Angelita has described. Commitment involves devoting oneself to promote the welfare and happiness of the other. It is a conscious attempt to tolerate a spouse's shortcomings and focus instead on strengths. It is sincerely trying to understand and meet the needs of another.

Commitment involves a decision to be involved with someone and to participate fully in making the relationship with that person as positive and fulfilling as possible. It is a decision to be 100 percent for that person and to be devoted to his or her welfare regardless of whether his or her behavior is good or bad.

Commitment is essential to the very first step of giving the blessing – making the decision to be a source of blessing to your spouse. And commitment is what is needed to carry through with bestowing the blessing.

Commitment is a willingness to love and a promise to love. It is a kind of love, which is the foundation upon which all lasting relationships are based.

In the garden of Arbor Lodge, home of J. Sterling Morton, who is the father of Arbor Day, there is a monument with the following poem. It expresses the blessing of commitment love very well:

Time flies.
Flowers die.
New days.
New ways.
Love stays.

BON VOYAGE

You are about to finish reading this book. Think of it not as the ending but the beginning. Today is the beginning of the rest of your voyage together. Your marriage is a living, unfolding adventure. It is a voyage that you can creatively chart for success. It is our hope that the principles shared by the many successful couples, upon which this book is based, will be beacons to show you the way to marriage happiness.

APPENDIX A

ASSESSING YOUR MARRIAGE

The quality of successful marriages can be broken down into 10 general categories as outlined below. Put an "S" for strength, beside the qualities you feel your marriage has achieved, and a "G" for growth, beside those qualities that are areas of potential growth. If the particular characteristic does not apply to your marriage or is not a characteristic important to you, put an "NA" for not applicable.

By doing this exercise, couples will be able to identify those areas they would like to work on together to improve and those areas of strength that will serve as the foundation for their growth and positive change together.

THE MARRIAGE ASSESSMENT TOOL

INTIMACY

1. ____We are very close to each other.
2. ____We trust each other.

3. ____We are honest and truthful (and kind).
4. ____We avoid playing mind games and trying to manipulate each other.
5. ____We consistently express an unconditional love for each other.
6. ____We love each other in the good times and the bad times.
7. ____We feel safe to be "ourselves" with each other.
8. ____We do not pretend with each other.
9. ____We feel psychologically comfortable with each other.
10. ___We can talk with each other about anything.
11. ___We avoid being judgmental and critical.
12. ___We are supportive of each other.
13. ___We consistently try to see things from each other's point of view.
14. ___We show respect and consideration to each other.
15. ___We are "always there" for each other.
16. ___We take care of each other and help each other.
17. ___Give an overall rating (S or G) of *intimacy in* your marriage.

COMMUNICATION

18. ____We allow time for communication (conversations, discussions).
19. ____We have positive communication.
20. ____We listen to each other.
21. ____We check the meaning of messages (give feedback, seek clarification).
22. ____We avoid sarcasm.
23. ____We are good, attentive listeners in our marriage communication.
24. ____We are sensitive to each other's non-verbal behavior and voice tone.
25. ____We often sit down and talk with each other in a relaxed manner.
26. ____We share many common interests.
27. ____We participate in several fun activities together.

28. _____We avoid blaming each other.
29. _____We are committed to promoting the welfare and happiness of each other.
30. _____We avoid trying to intimidate each other (temper tantrums, ridicule, threats).
31. _____We share our feelings with each other.
32. _____We refrain from "put-downs".
33. _____We consistently communicate messages of appreciation and encouragement to each other.
34. _____Give an overall rating (S or G) of *communication* in your marriage.

RESOLVING CONFLICT

35. _____We deal with conflict issues one at a time.
36. _____We are specific when dealing with conflict issues.
37. _____We avoid actions and words that would be emotionally devastating to each other.
38. _____We seek to understand and accept our differences.
39. _____We deal with disagreements promptly.
40. _____We avoid trying to change each other's values, attitudes, interests and personality characteristics.
41. _____We refrain from power struggles in our relationship.
42. _____We are not competitive with each other.
43. _____We are adaptable and willing to change our behavior when we have disagreements.
44. _____We are responsive to each other's concerns and frustrations.
45. _____We focus our energies on how we can best solve the problem when we experience conflict.
46. _____We refrain from attacking each other (blaming, accusations, name-calling) in conflict situations.
47. _____We avoid bringing up grievances from the past and using them against each other.
48. _____We take time to discuss conflict issues.

49. ____We discuss our problems at times that are unhurried and free of distractions.
50. ____We are patient with each other.
51. ____We are willing to make sacrifices for each other.
52. ____Give an overall rating (S or G) of *resolving conflict* in your marriage.

NAVIGATING DANGEROUS WATERS

53. ____We monitor carefully how our money is being spent.
54. ____We develop a clear plan for how our money is spent.
55. ____We establish priorities for how best to spend our money.
56. ____We maintain a temporary savings for emergencies.
57. ____We try to limit our credit debts to 15 – 20% of our take home pay (excluding mortgage payments).
58. ____We use a budget to help achieve our financial goals and manage resources.
59. ____We each consider our in-laws as family.
60. ____We each enjoy positive relationships with our in-laws.
61. ____We focus on the strengths of our in-laws.
62. ____We avoid concentrating on what our in-laws do that irritates us.
63. ____We respect the differences between us and our in-laws.
64. ____We never give up on each other.
65. ____We build up each other's self-esteem.
66. ____We keep a sense of adventure in our relationship.
67. ____We keep romance in our relationship by doing such things as writing love notes or sending flowers.
68. ____We go out on dates with each other.
69. ____We spend a lot of relaxed unhurried time together.
70. ____Give an overall rating (S or G) of *navigating dangerous waters.*

WEATHERING THE STORMS OF LIFE

71. _____We communicate with each other during tough times.

72. _____We avoid leaving each other to deal with a crisis alone.

73. _____We look for the good in the midst of a crisis.

74. _____We work together to face the challenges of crises.

75. _____We support each other emotionally in crisis situations.

76. _____We seek help from friends, church, and neighbors during crises.

77. _____We call on spiritual resources (God's help, faith, hope) in time of crises.

78. _____We see opportunities for personal and marriage growth in crisis situations.

79. _____We use good communication to share feelings and to solve problems.

80. _____We are flexible and adaptable.

81. _____We have a deep commitment to love and support each other in the bad times as well as the good times.

82. _____We help each other deal with problems.

83. _____We look for opportunities to produce something good out of a difficult situation.

84. _____When one of us is "down" the other gives encouragement and hope.

85. _____When we are in a crisis we set specific goals and then work together to meet those goals.

86. _____Give an overall rating (S or G) of *weathering the storms of life.*

DEVELOPING A GREAT SEXUAL RELATIONSHIP

87. _____We have a positive, loving, total relationship.

88. _____We are responsive to each other's needs.

89. _____We can trust each other.

90. _____In our sexual relationship we concentrate on giving and experiencing pleasure rather than being preoccupied with our sexual performance.

91. ____We purposely plan our sexual interactions at times when we are least likely to be fatigued or distracted.
92. ____We avoid becoming indifferent or neglectful of each other because of preoccupation with other areas of our lives.
93. ____We avoid criticizing and putting each other down.
94. ____We avoid sarcasm with each other.
95. ____We spend a lot of time talking with each other.
96. ____We spend a lot of time participating in fun activities together.
97. ____We are honest with each other.
98. ____We are psychologically comfortable with each other.
99. ____We refrain from being competitive with each other.
100. ___We build up each other's self-confidence.
101. ___We express appreciation to each other often.
102. ___We have a high commitment to each other.
103. ___We communicate with each other concerning specific sexual behavior we find enjoyable.
104. ___We are aware of some of the differences in the sexual response cycle of men and women.
105. ___Give an overall rating (S or G) of *developing a great sexual relationship.*

SPIRITUAL WELLNESS

106. ___We believe that God has a purpose for our lives.
107. ___Our spiritual faith helps us to successfully deal with problems.
108. ___We practice the art of "being still" (taking the time to see God's beauty and love all about us).
109. ___We have a great determination to work our problems out.
110. ___We avoid giving in to discouragement.
111. ___We never give up on each other.
112. ___We draw on the strength of God to forgive each other and ourselves (in little things and big things).
113. ___We regularly provide happy, joyful experiences for each other.

114. ___We believe that God watches over and guides our marriage.
115. ___We are patient with each other.
116. ___We have an outlook on life that is optimistic and hopeful.
117. ___We praise God for his love and involvement in our marriage.
118. ___We spend time each day in prayer.
119. ___We have an inner peace in difficult times because of our relationship with God.
120. ___We attend worship services together.
121. ___We have moral values that guide us (honesty, responsibility, kindness).
122. ___We apply our spiritual values to everyday life.
123. ___Give an overall rating (S or G) of *spiritual wellness*.

GIVING THE BLESSING

124. ___We give each other unconditional acceptance.
125. ___We make each other feel loved and lovable.
126. ___We make each other feel desirable.
127. ___We have made the decision to be a source of blessing to each other.
128. ___We consistently try to increase each other's happiness.
129. ___We consistently attempt to meet each other's needs.
130. ___We avoid being self-centered in our marriage relationship.
131. ___We give each other caring touches (a kiss, holding hands, and encouraging hand on the shoulder).
132. ___We verbally communicate high regard for each other.
133. ___We avoid focusing on each other's shortcomings.
134. ___We consistently express genuine appreciation to each other.
135. ___We share a common vision for our marriage.
136. ___We have a vision of a positive, special future for each other.
137. ___We believe in each other.
138. ___We make our marriage relationship a top priority with respect to how we invest our time and energy.
139. ___We have made the decision to love each other in bad times as well as good times.

140. ___We will do whatever it takes to love and bless each other.
141. ___Give an overall rating (S or G) of *giving the blessing* in your marriage.

APPENDIX B

A MARRIAGE SUCCESS ACTION PLAN

Your marriage may be great. You can make it even better! Perhaps at the present time your marriage is characterized by serious problems and does not reflect the high degree of success that you desire. If so, please don't be discouraged. Seeds of growth and success are at your disposal. Regardless of whether your marriage is happy or unhappy, marriage success can be yours. You can change the situation and make your marriage relationship better. People can change when they are willing to work at it.

What do you want your marriage to become in the future? Visualize what you want to see happen in your relationship. Write it down. Develop your own vision statement for your marriage. Encourage your spouse to do the same. Discuss your separate visions. Are there areas you can agree upon? Decide on some goals. Plan how you can work toward them. Be patient with yourself and your spouse. Be kind.

It may be helpful for you to develop a marriage success action plan revolving around the 10 beacons or qualities characterizing our successful couples. Try it! Your marriage success action plan can be an important aid in helping your marriage success to become a reality. It can be a seed which promotes the growth of your relationship into a "Magnificent Marriage".

MARRIAGE SUCCESS ACTION PLAN

BEACON TO SUCCESS: *EXPERIENCING INTIMACY*
What I want to happen: _____

_____

How I am going to do it (my strategies): _____

_____

Specific time I will start: _____

BEACON TO SUCCESS: *ENHANCING GOOD COMMUNICA-TION*
What I want to happen: _____

_____

How I am going to do it (my strategies): _____

_____

Specific time I will start: _____

BEACON TO SUCCESS: *KEEPING ROMANCE IN YOUR MARRIAGE*
What I want to happen: _____

_____

How I am going to do it (my strategies): _____

_____

Specific time I will start: _____

BEACON TO SUCCESS: *RESOLVING CONFLICT*

What I want to happen: _____

_____

How I am going to do it (my strategies): _____

_____

Specific time I will start: _____

BEACON TO SUCCESS: *OVERCOMING CHRONIC STRESS AND HASSLES*

What I want to happen: _____

How I am going to do it (my strategies): _____

_____

Specific time I will start: _____

BEACON TO SUCCESS: *NAVIGATING DANGEROUS WATERS*

Managing Finances
Loving Your In-laws
*Overcoming Addictions**
Affair-Proofing Your Marriage

What I want to happen: _____

_____

How I am going to do it (my strategies): _____

_____

Specific time I will start: _____

BEACON TO SUCCESS: *WEATHERING THE STORMS OF LIFE*

What I want to happen: _____

_____

How I am going to do it (my strategies): _____

_____

Specific time I will start: _____

BEACON TO SUCCESS: *DEVELOPING A GREAT SEXUAL RELA- TIONSHIP*

What I want to happen: _____

_____

How I am going to do it (my strategies): _____

_____

Specific time I will start: _____

BEACON TO SUCCESS: *NURTURING SPIRITUAL WELLNESS*

What I want to happen: _____

_____

How I am going to do it (my strategies): _____

_____

Specific time I will start: _____

BEACON TO SUCCESS: *GIVING THE BLESSING*

What I want to happen: _____

_____

How I am going to do it (my strategies): _____

_____

Specific time I will start: _____

*Overcoming addictions may not be applicable for your marriage. However, remember that addictions may include many areas, including television, the computer, and even work.

APPENDIX C

PUTTING IT INTO ACTION

Chapter 1
EXPERIENCING INTIMACY

Don't You Agree?

Does your spouse agree that the following items are what intimacy is all about?

1. Making up after a sharp disagreement.
2. Cuddling in bed at night before going to sleep.
3. Crying together at a funeral.
4. Sharing your innermost thoughts and feelings with each other.
5. Working as a team on household chores.
6. Thoughtful words or gestures
7. Being respected.
8. Trusting each other.
9. Feeling unconditionally accepted.

10. Laughing together.

Share the above list with each other and talk about the importance of each item to you.

What Do You Know?

Lasting marriages are built on a solid foundation of COMMITMENT. They don't just happen; they grow and develop & mature. An atmosphere that is conducive to growth involves two people who have a determination to know each other and a willingness to be known by each other.

How much do you know about your mate?

- FOR STARTERS…Do you know your spouse's:
  Birthplace?
  Mother's maiden name?
  Favorite food?
  Most enjoyable hobby?
  Color of eyes?
  Latest triumph?

- TAPPING THE MIND…
  How would your spouse complete the following:
  1. My mate's most endearing quality is…
  2. Our marriage…
  3. My greatest strength…
  4. My greatest need…
  5. Our future together…

Chapter 2
ENHANCING GOOD COMMUNICATION

Creating A Verbal Bouquet

Put together the following, then set aside a specific time and place to "present" your bouquet.

- Tell a humorous story (embarrassing moment, a clean joke, etc.).
- Clip a funny cartoon.
- Make a list of five compliments for your mate.
- Share a fantasy (what you would do with a billion dollars, how you would use 3 wishes from a genie, etc.)
- Write a brief love note to your mate telling why you are glad to be married to him/her.
- Record the love note on a cassette tape.
- Draw a picture of a favorite memory that involves your mate.

Make A Wish

Wives: Make a list of three things you would like to see your husband do.

Husbands: Make a list of three things you would like to see your wife do.

Set aside a specific time and place.

Share your list by taking turns.

Each share one wish and let your partner respond by asking for clarification and then confirming what he/she heard by saying, "I hear you saying…"

Continue this process until all six wishes are expressed and confirmed.

Chapter 3
KEEPING ROMANCE IN YOUR MARRIAGE

How Do I Love Thee?
1. What first attracted you to your mate?
2. What do you admire most about your mate today?
3. How has your mate helped you become a better person?
4. How have you helped your mate become a better person?
5. When are you most satisfied with your mate?
6. Name two goals that you and your mate share.

7. What is the nicest thing your mate has ever said to you?
8. What is the nicest thing you have ever said to your mate?
9. When was the last time you said it?
10. What could you do to show your mate your commitment to your marriage?

Looking for a Few Good Men & Women

1. Who is the married couple (living or not) that I admire the most?
2. Why do I admire them?
3. Describe their marriage.
4. What attitudes/actions toward his wife make that husband a good husband?
5. What attitudes/actions toward her husband make that wife a good wife?
6. What do I value most in my marriage?
7. What is keeping me married to my mate?
8. In my life with my mate, what brings the greatest joy?
9. If someone else selected us as the married couple they most admire, what attitudes/actions would they cite in our marriage?
10. What quality does my mate possess that I would never change?

Chapter 4
RESOLVING CONFLICT

Odds In Our Favor

At the University of Washington researchers have discovered some numbers that may help couples stay happily married. Findings show that for every negative comment and/or action displayed there need to be five positive comments and/or actions displayed by the offender in order to maintain a positive couple relationship.

When disagreements arise, remember this 5-to-1 ratio. If you apply it, odds are your marriage will remain strong.

Five Steps To An Apology
1. Identify the hurt you have caused.
2. Isolate what you did to cause the hurt.
3. Seek out an opportunity to discuss the problem with your mate.
4. Ask for forgiveness.
5. Follow through with a hug and a kiss.

Chapter 5
OVERCOMING CHRONIC STRESS AND HASSLES

A Friendly Reminder
A. List the ten activities in which you are involved consistently that take up most of your time.

1.	6.
2.	7.
3.	8.
4.	9.
5.	10.

B. List five important goals that you have set to achieve in the next five years.

1.
2.
3.
4.
5.

C. Review list A in light of your goals. Put a plus (+) sign in front of each activity that is helping you toward achieving your goal(s). Put a minus (-) sign in front of each activity that is hindering you from achieving your goal(s).

NOTE: *Occasionally we each need to be reminded where we are headed and how well we are doing to get there. Be willing to make* *adjustments as needed in your activities and/or your goals.*

Taking A Ten-Minute Vacation

Both of you think of the "perfect" vacation. With money being no object, describe how you will travel, where you will go, and what your itinerary will be. What will be some of your favorite restaurants and meals? Will you go shopping, play sports, or attend a concert?

One at a time, tell about your vacation.

Chapter 6
NAVIGATING DANGEROUS WATERS:
How to Manage Finances
How to Love Your In-laws

Reframing Hurtful Treatment

There are times in married life when our mate or an in-law does or says something that hurts us deeply. For some, this is not an easy thing to get over. One strategy that can help us work through the hurt is reframing.

To reframe is to see something positive in an otherwise negative situation. For example, after a fierce argument, a young husband's wife of six months has just left him and gone to her mother's. The young husband may reframe this event by observing, "At least I know she is safe at her mom's house; I can call her in a little bit."

Another example is a husband has just told his wife that she is overweight. The wife may reframe the hurtful remark by thinking, "I am glad he is able to tell me how he feels; this will encourage me to get the exercise I need."

A more dramatic example is a husband who leaves his wife for another woman. The wife may reframe this devastating experience by reasoning, "I am just thankful that this occurred while I am young and have no children."

Hurt feelings can result from good intentions. Jane's mother-in-law, Sue, openly disagreed with the method Jane used to discipline her child. That hurt Jane's feelings, but she reframed the experience by adopting this attitude, "Sue loves my children so much that she was willing to openly disagree with me."

Reframing is an attitude and a determination to see good even when things seem bad.

What We're Headed For

A shared activity that is a powerful solidifier of marriages is GOAL-SETTING. Setting goals together keeps the couple "on the same page," working in the same direction as a team. Also, goals give a couple something to look forward to together. Goals provide a sense of positive development for any marriage.

As a couple, fill in the sections below with your goals for the next six months.

FINANCIAL GOALS

1.

2.

3.

FAMILY GOALS

1.

2.

3.

SPIRITUAL GOALS

1.

2.

3.

Chapter 7

NAVIGATING DANGEROUS WATERS:

How Couples Overcome Addictions
How to "Affair-Proof" Your Marriage

WHO GROWS THERE?

How I See You \ How I See Me	I Have Worth	I Have No Worth
You Have Worth	Produces: TRUST CONFIDENCE SUPPORT RESPECT AFFECTION Outcome: We BOTH thrive	Produces: DEPENDENCE RESENTMENT INFERIORITY LACK OF ASSERTIVENESS DEFENSIVENESS Outcome: I degenerate You thrive
You Have No Worth	Produces: SUPERIORITY CRITICISM DEMANDS THREATS COMPLAINTS Outcome: I thrive You degenerate	Produces: HOPELESSNESS WITHDRAWAL AIMLESSNESS LACK OF COMMITMENT UNFAITHFULNESS Outcome: We BOTH degenerate

Renewing Your Marriage Commitment

Remember the vows you made to each other the day you were married. Are you still as committed to your mate today as you were then?

Would you both be willing to repeat the following vows to each other? If you both are willing, designate a specific time and a secluded place to say the following words to each other.

HUSBAND: "I, (YOUR NAME), continue to take you (WIFE'S NAME), to be my wedded companion, through all of life. I pledge my faithfulness and my love, to you and you alone."

WIFE: "I, (YOUR NAME), continue to take you (HUSBAND'S NAME), to be my wedded companion, through all of life. I pledge my faithfulness and my love, to you and you alone."

Now, kiss each other to seal the renewal of your commitment.

Chapter 8
WEATHERING THE STORMS OF LIFE

Does This Describe Us?

How are we as a couple like the following statement?
Not At All Like Us = 1
Sometimes Like Us = 2
Almost Always Like Us = 3

1.	We look for something good even in bad situations.	1	2	3
2.	We stick together through good times and bad times.	1	2	3
3.	We have a willingness to seek outside help if needed.	1	2	3
4.	We regularly carve out time to be together	1	2	3
5.	We are optimistic about our future together.	1	2	3
6.	We have friends and relatives who would help us through a crisis.	1	2	3
7.	When we are faced with difficulties, we discuss our options and agree on a solution.	1	2	3
8.	We can count on each other.	1	2	3
9.	We do not take each other for granted.	1	2	3

10. We usually agree on what is important
    to our relationship.   1   2   3

Strategy Planner

I believe my partner's ability to be supportive would be a: *(circle the appropriate number.)*

      1   2   3   4   5   6   7   8   9   10

   Weakest   Strongest

I believe my ability to be supportive would be a: *(circle the appropriate number.)*

      1   2   3   4   5   6   7   8   9   10

   Weakest   Strongest

Based on my perceptions of my mate's communication skills and my communication skills, I plan to:

❑ Increase my assertiveness   ❑ Decrease my assertiveness
❑ Increase my responsiveness   ❑ Decrease my responsiveness
❑ Not change my assertiveness   ❑ Not change my responsiveness

I plan to reach my goal by (list your action steps):

_____

_____

_____

_____

_____

_____

_____

_____

_____

_____

_____

_____

_____

Chapter 9
DEVELOPING A GREAT
SEXUAL RELATIONSHIP

Evaluating Myself as a Lover

Evaluate yourself by placing an "X" on each line at the point that best shows how you feel about your own skills right now as a lover of your spouse.

1. I see possibilities weekly to fulfill my spouse's needs to be accepted and valued.

_____

Rarely   Consistently

2. I show my spouse respect and kindness.

_____

Rarely   Consistently

3. I express verbally my love and appreciation for my spouse and display that love by opening my life to him/her.

_____

Rarely   Consistently

4. I initiate romance rather than waiting for my spouse to reach out to me.

_____

Rarely   Consistently

5. I work to help my spouse realize his/her full potential as a human being.

_____

Rarely   Consistently

Playing the Right Notes

From the following list of 14 qualities, select one each day this week that reminds you of your mate and use it to compose a short note of appreciation or admiration to your spouse. Place the notes where your mate can easily find them.

1. Affectionate
2. Attractive
3. Considerate
4. Creative
5. Dependable
6. Determined
7. Forgiving
8. Fun
9. Funny
10. Generous
11. Hardworking
12. Patient
13. Spiritual
14. Willing to serve

Sample note: Dear Sherrie,

I am really a lucky guy to have a wife who is so hardworking. I appreciate all you do for the kids and me to make our lives comfortable and happy.

I love you,
Donnie

Chapter 10
NURTURING SPIRITUAL WELLNESS

Assessing Your Relationship with God
In The Present

Strengths of my relationship with God	Ways my relationship with God needs to grow
1.	1.
2.	2.
3.	3.
4.	4.
5.	5.

In The Future

Opportunities to grow closer to God	Threats to my relationship with God
1.	1.
2.	2.
3.	3.
4.	4.
5.	5.

One Another

Consider together the following "one another passages" contained in the New Testament. Circle the "S" if you consider this an area of strength in your marriage relationship. Circle the "G" if you consider this an area of needed growth in your marriage relationship.

Love one another (John 13:34)	S	G
Be devoted to one another (Romans 12:10)	S	G
Honor one another (Romans 12:10)	S	G
Accept one another (Romans 15:7)	S	G
Serve one another (Galatians 5:13)	S	G
Bear one another's burdens (Galatians 6:2)	S	G
Submit to one another (Ephesians 5:21)	S	G
Forgive one another (Colossians 3:13)	S	G
Encourage one another (1 Thessalonians 5:11)	S	G

Chapter 11
GIVING THE BLESSING

Review and Renew

Individually respond to the following items:

- Select the word that best describes the communication lifestyle of you and your spouse:
  1. Great
  2. Good
  3. O.K.

4. Lacking
5. Pitiful

- Which word will your spouse select?
- Write down one thing you can do to improve the communication lifestyle of you and your spouse.
- On a 3 X 5 card, write down a commitment statement and sign it. "I will immediately begin to improve my communication with my spouse by doing the following…"
- Now, set aside a specific time and place to discuss each other's responses. At the end of your discussion, decide on a specific date and time for a follow-up meeting (about a week later). At that meeting review your progress as a couple and renew your commitment to improve your communication together.

"We Always"

Can you and your spouse recall the family traditions and celebrations that you both experienced while growing up?

Complete the following sentences together as the two of you remember.

At mealtimes we always used to……
On birthdays we always used to……
On Sundays we always used to……
At Easter we always used to……
At Halloween we always used to…..
At Thanksgiving we always used to……
At Christmas we always used to……
On New Year's Day we always used to……
For summer vacation we always used to……
At bedtime we always used to……

Which of the above childhood traditions have you and your spouse established in your family together?

APPENDIX D

RESOURCES TO HELP YOUR MARRIAGE BECOME MAGNIFICENT

WEB SITES FOR COUPLES

Center for Relationship Development: Les & Leslie Parrott
www.realrelationships.com

Current Movie & Video Reviews for Parents
www.familystyle.com/index.htm

Directory of organizations dealing with all kinds of addictions.
http://4addictions.4anything.com

Family Dynamics Institute
www.familydynamics.net

Gambler's Anonymous
P. O. Box 17173
Los Angeles, CA 9017
(213) 386-8789
http:www.gamblersanonymous.org

National Center for Fathering
www.fathers.com

National Fatherhood Initiative
www.fatherhood.org

Parent's Place
www.family.org/pplace.

Finance Center.com
www.financenter.com
Covers home & auto loans, saving, investing & retirement,
insurance & credit cards. Includes info, advice & best deals.

Investorguide.com
www.investorguide.com
Directory of investing & personal finance sites, plus weekly
newsletter & feature articles.

Quicken.com
www.quicken.com
News & feature stories on personal finance & investing, plus
stock quotes and tools such as a mortgage calculator.

ENRICHMENT PROGRAMS FOR COUPLES

Association for Couples for Marriage Enrichment (ACME)

ACME National Office
P. O. Box 10596
Winston Salem, NC 27108
(800) 634-8325

American Association of Marital and Family Therapy (AAMFT)

1133 15th St. NW, Suite 300
Washington, D.C. 20005
(202) 452-0109

Family Dynamics Institute

P. O. Box 211668
Augusta, GA 30917-1668
(800) 650-9995

Growing Together Program

Life Innovations, Inc.
PREPARE/ENRICH
P. O. Box 190
Minneapolis, MN 55440-0190
(800) 331-1661

Marriage Savers

Michael & Harriet McManus
9500 Michaels Court
Bethesda, MD 20817-2214
(301) 469-5870

National Marriage Encounter

4704 Jamerson Place
Orlando, FL 32807
(800) 828-3351

Prevention & Relationship Enhancement Program (PRE)

Dr. Howard Markman
Center for Marriage & Family Studies
P. O. Box 102530
Denver, CO 80250-2530
(303) 759-9931

RESOURCES FOR COUPLES

American Association of Christian Counselors
P.O. Box 739, Forest, VA 24551-9973
804-384-0564

Clearinghouse on Family Violence Information
P. O. Box 1182, Washington, DC 20013
703-385-7565

Cloverdale Center for Family Strengths
Faulkner University
5345 Atlanta Highway, Montgomery, AL
334-386-7576

Eating Disorders
Remuda Ranch – 800-445-1900
Jack Burden Rd., Box 2481, Wickenburg, AZ 85358

Family Dynamics Institute
P. O. Box 211668, Augusta, GA 30917-1668
706-855-9900

Missing Children HELP Center
410 Ware Blvd., Ste. 400, Tampa, FL. 33619
800-872-5437

National Coalition Against Pornography
800 Compton Rd., Ste. 9224, Cincinnati, OH 45231
513-521-6227

National Council on Alcoholism and Drug Abuse
87909 Manchester Road, St. Louis, MO 63144
314-962-3456

National Domestic Violence Hotline
800-333-SAFE

National PTA Drug and Alcohol Abuse
Prevention Project
330 North Wabash Avenue, Suite 2100, Chicago, IL 60611-3690
312-670-6782

National Runaway Switchboard and Suicide
Hotline 800-621-4000 or 312-880-9860

Parents' Resource Institute for Drug Education, Inc. (PRIDE)
50 Hurt Plaza, Suite 210, Atlanta, GA 30303
404-577-4500
800-677-7433

Resolve
S. Water Street, Arlington, MA 02174
617-643-2424
(provides phone counseling/referral for persons experiencing infertility.)

Resources for Living
2807 Manchaca Road, Austin, TX 78704
800-678-2212

The Alzheimer's & Dementia
H.E.L.P. LINE
1-800-457-5679

BOOKS FOR COUPLES

J. Beam. *Becoming One.* West Monroe, LA: Howard Publishing, 1999.

L. Burkett. *The Complete Financial Guide for Young Couples.* Wheaton, IL: Victor Books, 1989.

S. Covey. *The 7 Habits of Highly Effective Families.* New York: Golden Books, 1997.

J. Gottman. *Why Marriages Succeed or Fail.* New York, NY: Simon & Schuster, 1994.

W. Harley. *Give and Take: The Secret to Marital Compatibility.* Grand Rapids, MI: Fleming H. Revell, 1996.

M. McManus. *Marriage Savers.* Grand Rapids, MI: Zondervan, 1993.

J. Rosemond. *A Family of Value.* Kansas City, MO: Andrews & McMeel, 1996.

G. Smalley & J. Trent. *The Gift of the Blessing.* Nashville, TN: Thomas Nelson, 1993.

N. Stinnett, N. Stinnett, J. Beam & A. Beam. *Fantastic Families.* West Monroe, LA: Howard Publishing, 1999.

NOTES

INTRODUCTION:
A LIGHTHOUSE FOR YOUR MARRIAGE VOYAGE

1. N. Stinnett, N. Stinnett, J. Beam, and A. Beam. *Fantastic Families.* West Monroe, Louisiana: Howard Publishing, 1999.

CHAPTER 1.
EXPERIENCING INTIMACY

1. N. Stinnett, J. Walters, and N. Stinnett. *Relationships in Marriage and the Family.* New York: Macmillan, 1991.

CHAPTER 2.
NURTURING GOOD COMMUNICATION

1. N. Stinnett, J. Walters, and N. Stinnett. *Relationships in Marriage and the Family.* New York: Macmillan, 1991.
    D. Tanner. *You Just Don't Understand: Men and Women in Conversation.* London: Virago, 1990.
    V. Wheeless, W. Zakahi, and M. Chan. "A Test of Self-Disclosure Based on Perceptions of a Target's Loneliness and Gender Orientation." *Communication Quarterly,* 36, 109-121, 1988.
    D. Knox and C. Schacht. *Choices in Relationships.* Belmont, CA: Wadsworth/Thomson Learning, 2000.

2. S. Wahlroos. *Family Communication.* New York: New American Library, 1983.

CHAPTER 3.
RESOLVING CONFLICT

1. D. Knox and C. Schacht. *Choices in Relationships*. Belmont, CA: Wadsworth/Thomson Learning, 2000.

2. H. Weingarten and S. Leas. "Levels of Marital Conflict Model: A Guide To Assessment and Intervention in Troubled Marriages." *American Journal of Orthopsychiatry*, 57, 407-417, 1987.

CHAPTER 4.
KEEPING ROMANCE IN YOUR MARRIAGE

1. T. Kinkade. *Simpler Times*. Eugene, Oregon: Harvest House, 1996.

CHAPTER 5.
OVERCOMING CHRONIC STRESS AND HASSLES

1. *Statistical Abstract of the United States: 1999 (119th edition)*. Washington D.C.: U.S. Bureau of the Census.
   M. Perry-Jenkins and K. Folk. "Class, Couples and Conflict: Effects of the Division of Labor on Assessments of Marriage in Dual-Earner Families." *Journal of Marriage and the Family*, 56:65-180, 1994.

2. A. Lindbergh. *Gift From the Sea*. New York: Pantheon, 1975.

CHAPTER 6.
NAVIGATING DANGEROUS WATERS:
How to Manage Finances
How to Love Your In-laws

1. D. Olson and J. DeFrain. *Marriage and the Family: Diversity and Strengths (3rd edition).* Mountain View, CA: Mayfield Publishing Company, 2000.

2. *Statistical Abstract of the United States: 1999 (119th edition).* Washington, D. C.: U. S. Bureau of the Census.

3. N. Stinnett, J. Walters, and N. Stinnett. *Relationships in Marriage and the Family.* New York: Macmillan, 1991.

CHAPTER 7.
NAVIGATING DANGEROUS WATERS:
How Couples Overcome Addictions
How to "Affair-Proof" Your Marriage

1. R. Turner and D. Lloyd. "Lifetime Traumas and Mental Health: The Significance of Cumulative Adversity." *Journal of Health and Social Adversity,* 36: 360-76, 1995.

2. P. Amato and S. Rogers. "A Longitudinal Study of Marital Problems and Subsequent Divorce." *Journal of Marriage and the Family,* 59: 612-24, 1997.

3. N. Stinnett, J. Walters, and N. Stinnett. *Relationships in Marriage and the Family.* New York: Macmillan, 1991.

CHAPTER 8.
WEATHERING THE STORMS OF LIFE

1. N. Stinnett, N. Stinnett, J. Beam, and A. Beam. *Fantastic Families. Six Steps to Make Your Family Stronger.* West Monroe, Louisiana: Howard Publishing, 1999.

CHAPTER 9.
DEVELOPING A GREAT SEXUAL RELATIONSHIP

1. N. Stinnett, J. Walters, and N. Stinnett. *Relationships in Marriage and the Family.* New York: Macmillan, 1991.
2. D. Knox and C. Schacht. *Choices in Relationships.* Belmont, CA: Wadsworth/Thomson Learning, 2000.

3. W. Masters, V. Johnson, and R. Kolodny. *Human Sexuality (5th edition).* New York: Harper Collins, 1995.

4. W. Masters and V. Johnson. *Human Sexual Response.* Little, Brown, 1996.

    W. Masters, V. Johnson, and R. Kolodny. *Human Sexuality (5th edition).* New York: Harper Collins, 1995.

CHAPTER 10.
NURTURING SPIRITUAL WELLNESS

1. I Corinthians 13: 4-8. *Holy Bible, New International Version.* International Bible Society, 1984.

2. E. Fromm. *The Art of Loving.* New York: Harper, 1956.

3. N. Stinnett, J. Walters, and N. Stinnett. *Relationships in Marriage and the Family.* New York: Macmillan, 1991.

4. Isaiah 41:10. *Holy Bible, New International Version.* International Bible Society, 1984.

5. Psalms 27:1. *Holy Bible. New International Version.* International Bible Society, 1984.

6. N. Stinnett, J. Walters, and N. Stinnett. *Relationships in Marriage and the Family.* New York: Macmillan, 1991.

7. H. Otto. *More Joy in Your Marriage.* New York: Hawthorn.

CHAPTER 11.
GIVING THE BLESSING

1. J. Eidsmoe. Columbus and Cortex, *Conquerors for Christ.* Green Forest, AR: New Leaf Press, p. 107, 1992.

2. G. Smalley and J. Trent. *The Gift of the Blessing.* Nashville, TN: Thomas Nelson, 1993.

3. N. Stinnett, N. Stinnett, and J. Walters. *Relationships in Marriage and the Family.* New York: Macmillan, 1991.

4. N. Stinnett, N. Stinnett, J. Beam, and A. Beam. *Fantastic Families.* West Monroe, Louisiana: Howard Publishing, 1999.